实用
英语口语
在专业领域成长

韩 艳◎著

吉林出版集团股份有限公司
全国百佳图书出版单位

图书在版编目 (CIP) 数据

实用英语口语 : 在专业领域成长 / 韩艳著 . -- 长春 : 吉林出版集团股份有限公司 , 2023.12

ISBN 978-7-5731-4238-2

Ⅰ . ①实… Ⅱ . ①韩… Ⅲ . ①英语－口语 Ⅳ . ① H319.9

中国国家版本馆 CIP 数据核字（2023）第 188865 号

实用英语口语：在专业领域成长

SHIYONG YINGYU KOUYU ZAI ZHUANYE LINGYU CHENGZHANG

著　　者：韩　艳
责任编辑：许　宁
封面设计：刘红刚
出　　版：吉林出版集团股份有限公司
发　　行：吉林出版集团外语教育有限公司
地　　址：吉林省长春市福祉大路 5788 号龙腾国际大厦 B 座 7 层
电　　话：总编办：0431-81629929
印　　刷：北京亚吉飞数码科技有限公司
版　　次：2023 年 12 月第 1 版
印　　次：2023 年 12 月第 1 次印刷
开　　本：710mm × 1000mm　1/16
印　　张：14.5
字　　数：160 千字

ISBN 978-7-5731-4238-2　　**定价**：56.00 元

举报电话：0431-81629929

Preface 前言

英语作为国际通用语言，在现实生活中的应用越来越广泛，各行各业都离不开英语，而英语口语能力也成为每个人提升核心竞争力、实现专业领域跨越式成长的必备技能之一。

但在日常生活和工作中，很多人无法自信开口说英语，更不能将英语运用到自己的专业领域来助力自己提升，对此苦恼不已。不必烦恼，本书将帮你解忧，带你突破英语口语，助你轻松变身英语达人，在专业领域不断提升和成长。

本书从商务活动到文化交流，从体育运动到前沿科技等，涵盖八大专业领域，囊括百余词汇和例句、几十个常见场景，为你全面剖析实用英语口语学习的技巧，助你快速掌握学习重点。

其中，本书收集的口语词汇基础实用、专业全面，帮助你由易到难、循序渐进地学习；精选的例句新颖地道、丰富灵活，供你在不同场合游刃有余地运用；设置的情景对话生动形象、贴近现实，激发你学习、模仿的兴趣，让你在实践中切实提升英语口语能力。

本书内容丰富翔实，语言通畅地道，英语氛围浓郁，英汉相互对照，便于读者阅读和理解，堪称一本专为不同专业领域英语口语学习者量身打造的英语宝典。

阅读本书，轻松消除对英语交流的恐惧，真正享受开口说英语的乐趣，并逐步实现在专业领域的成长与进步。

作　者

2023 年 6 月

Contents 目录

目 录

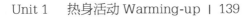

Chapter 8　前沿科技 | 193

参考文献 | 223

Chapter 1
商务活动

在经济全球化发展的今天，商务活动频繁。而在商务活动中，具备良好的英语口语能力至关重要，因为流利的口语能够对新品发布、产品展示、商务谈判以及合同签订等起到明显的助力作用，能够保障商务活动有效开展，促进商务活动的成功。

Unit 1

新品发布

New Product Launch

新品发布是企业推广和营销的重要环节，在这个环节中，英语口语发挥着重要的作用。使用流利、准确的英语口语发布新品，可以吸引全球观众，扩大产品的知名度和市场份额。下面就一起来学习一下相关的表达吧。

单词展示

launch [lɔːntʃ] *vt.* 发行

release [rɪˈliːs] *n.* 发布

announcement [əˈnaʊnsmənt] *n.* 宣布

unveil [ʌnˈveɪl] *v.* 揭幕

debut [ˈdeɪbjuː] *n.* 问世

premiere [ˈpremieə(r)] *n.* 首映式

smartphone [ˈsmɑːtfəʊn] *n.* 智能手机

presentation [ˌpreznˈteɪʃn] *n.* 介绍会

reveal [rɪˈviːl] *v.* 揭示

preview [ˈpriːvjuː] *n.* 预展

句子示范

The company plans to release a brand new smartphone next month.

公司计划在下个月发布一款全新的智能手机。

We are ready to bring our innovative products to market.

我们已经准备好将我们的创新产品推向市场。

The new product launch will be held in a large conference hall, and hundreds of media and industry insiders are expected to attend.

新品发布会将在大型会议厅举行，预计会有数百名媒体和业内人士参加。

The new product launch activities will include product demonstrations, expert lectures and user experience exchanges.

新品发布活动将包括产品演示、专家讲座和用户体验交流等环节。

C 公司要发布新品智能手表，Debby 作为记者，采访了产品经理 Alden。

D=Debby　　A=Alden

A: Our company is about to launch a brand new smartwatch.

D: That's so exciting! What makes this watch special?

A: It integrates the latest health monitoring technology, allowing real-time tracking of heart rate, blood pressure, and sleep quality. Moreover, it supports a smart voice assistant and seamless connectivity with smartphones.

D: That sounds great! When can we see the actual product?

A: The company plans to hold a grand product launch event next month, and all the features of this watch will be showcased, and people will have the opportunity to experience it firsthand.

D: That's wonderful! What highlights can we expect from the launch event?

A: Apart from the watch demonstration and feature presentation, we have invited industry experts to deliver on-site speeches, sharing insights into the future development trends of smart wearables. We have already extended invitations to representatives from some competitor companies. We aim to showcase our technological advantages and engage in in-depth discussions and competition with them.

D: That's fantastic! Will the event updates be shared on the company's social media and official website?

A: We will promptly provide relevant information and maintain smooth communication with users and potential customers.

D: Great. I believe this new product will be highly popular.

A: I look forward to witnessing our company achieving significant breakthroughs in the market once again!

A: 我们公司即将发布一款全新的智能手表。

D: 这太令人兴奋了！这款手表有什么特别之处呢？

A: 它集成了最新的健康监测技术，能够实时监测心率、血压和睡眠质量。而且，它还支持智能语音助手，可以与手机进行无缝连接。

D: 那听起来很不错！我们什么时候能看到实物呢？

A: 公司计划在下个月举行一场盛大的新品发布会，届时会展示这款手表的所有功能，并允许人们亲自体验。

D: 那真是太好了！这场发布会会有哪些亮点？

A: 除了手表的展示和功能介绍外，我们还邀请了行业内的专家进行现场演讲，分享智能穿戴设备的未来发展趋势。我们已经邀请了一些竞品公司的代表参加发布会。我们希望借此机会，展示我们的技术领先优势，并与他们进行深入的交流和竞争。

D: 太棒了！那到时候是否会在公司的社交媒体和官方网站上更新发布会的信息呢？

A: 我们会及时提供相关信息，并保持与用户和潜在客户的沟通畅通。

D: 好的。我相信这款新产品一定会大受欢迎。

A: 我期待见证我们公司在市场上再次取得巨大突破！

Unit 2

产品展示

Product Demonstration

产品展示是向目标受众展示产品功能和价值的重要环节。通过流利的英语口语，能够准确、生动地描述产品特点，更好地传达产品的竞争优势和独特卖点，有效吸引大众的注意力。下面就一起来学习相关的表达吧。

单词 展示

exhibition [ˌeksɪˈbɪʃn] *n.* 展览	display [dɪˈspleɪ] *n.* 陈列
showcase [ˈʃəʊkeɪs] *n.* 展示柜	demonstration [ˌdemənˈstreɪʃn] *n.* 示范，演示
booth [buːð] *n.* 展位	model [ˈmɒdl] *n.* 模型，样品
catalog [ˈkætəlɒg] *n.* 目录，目录册	showroom [ˈʃəʊruːm] *n.* 展览厅
feature [ˈfiːtʃər] *n.* 特点	advanced [ədˈvɑːnst] *adj.* 先进的

句子示范

The display area has a special display counter for customers to understand and experience our products.

展示区设有一个专门的展示柜台，供客户了解和体验我们的产品。

At the exhibition, we will showcase our product features and innovative designs.

展示会上，我们将展示我们的产品功能和创新设计。

We have prepared some product samples for customers to try by themselves.

我们准备了一些产品样本供客户亲自试用。

We will show our company’s latest technology and research and development achievements at the exhibition.

我们将在展示会上展示我们公司的最新技术和研发成果。

After the show, we will have a sales team on site to accept orders and provide after-sales service.

展示会结束后，我们将有销售团队在现场接受订单和提供售后服务。

A 公司最近正在举办产品展示会，在现场，A 公司工作人员 Anna 正与顾客 Mark 进行交流。

A=Anna　　M=Mark

A: Hello, welcome to our product showcase! I'm an employee of the floor-cleaning robot company. How can I assist you?

M: Hi! I'm interested in floor-cleaning robots, but I'm not familiar with the different models and their features. Could you introduce your products to me?

A: Certainly! Our company offers several models of floor-cleaning robots, each with unique features and capabilities. Let me introduce our most popular model to you, the RT 5000. It's our flagship product, known for its outstanding cleaning performance and intelligent functions.

M: That sounds great! Could you tell me some of its main features?

A: Absolutely! The RT 5000 utilizes advanced floor-cleaning technology, allowing it to effortlessly clean various surfaces, including hardwood floors, carpets, and tiles. It's equipped with a powerful vacuum cleaner that effectively captures dust, hair, pet fur, and other debris.

Additionally, it has an automatic obstacle avoidance function that enables it to navigate around obstacles, ensuring comprehensive coverage during cleaning.

M: That's really impressive! I have a few more questions. How is the battery life of this robot?

A: The RT 5000 has an impressive battery life. It can work continuously for over 8 hours on a full charge.

M: Great! Thank you for your assistance. I will carefully consider it.

A: 您好，欢迎光临我们的产品展示现场！我是扫地机公司的员工，有什么可以帮您的吗？

M: 你好！我对扫地机很感兴趣，但是对于不同型号和功能还不太了解。能给我介绍一下你们的产品吗？

A: 当然可以！我们公司有几款不同型号的扫地机，每个型号都有不同的功能和特点。让我为您介绍一下最受欢迎的型号——RT 5000。它是我们的旗舰产品，具有卓越的清扫性能和智能功能。

M: 听起来很不错！能告诉我一些它的主要特点吗？

A: 当然！RT 5000 采用先进的扫地技术，可以轻松清扫各种地面，包括硬地板、地毯和瓷砖。它还配备了强大的吸尘器，能够有效吸入灰尘、头发和宠物毛发等杂物。此外，它还具有自动避障功能，可以在遇到障碍物时自动绕过，保证全面的清扫覆盖面。

M: 这真是太棒了！我还有一些问题想问一下。这款扫地机的电池寿命如何?

A: RT 5000 的电池寿命非常可观，一次充满电可以连续工作 8 小时以上。

M: 好的，谢谢你的帮助！我会仔细考虑的。

Unit 3

商务谈判

Business Negotiation

商务谈判对于商业交流和决策来说至关重要，流利的英语口语有助于清晰表达立场、理解对方观点和谈判目标，提高谈判效果，实现谈判共赢。下面就一起来学习一下相关的表达吧。

单词展示

negotiation [nɪˌɡəʊʃiˈeɪʃn] *n.* 谈判，协商

agreement [əˈɡriːmənt] *n.* 协议

contract [ˈkɒntrækt] *n.* 合同

proposal [prəˈpəʊzl] *n.* 提议

offer [ˈɒfə(r)] *n.* 提议

counteroffer [ˈkaʊntə(r)ˌɔːfə(r)] *n.* 还盘

beneficial [ˌbenɪˈfɪʃl] *adj.* 有益的

assess [əˈses] *vt.* 评估

bargaining [ˈbɑːɡənɪŋ] *n.* 讨价还价

concession [kənˈseʃn] *n.* 让步，妥协

句子示范

We would like to be able to include some special terms and conditions in the contract.

我们希望能够在合同中加入一些特殊条款和条件。

We hope to reach a mutually beneficial and win-win agreement to ensure that both parties can benefit.

我们希望能够达成一个互利双赢的协议，确保双方都能得到利益。

Please explain some terms in the contract. We have some questions.

请解释一下合同中的某些条款，我们有一些疑问。

We need to negotiate a suitable delivery date and shipping method.

我们需要商议一个合适的交货日期和运输方式。

Ellen 是 A 公司的销售经理，来到 B 公司与其采购经理 Hazel 谈判采购价格。

E=Ellen　　H=Hazel

E: Hello, I am here on behalf of our company for this business negotiation. I'm Ellen, the Sales Manager of Company A.

H: Hello. Nice to meet you. I'm Hazel.

E: We have received the purchasing price list from your company, and we have assessed the types and quantities of products.

H: Thank you for your feedback. So, what are your thoughts on our pricing?

E: The pricing you proposed is relatively reasonable compared to the market. However, we would like to have some room for negotiation.

H: I understand your perspective. We also hope to reach a mutually beneficial agreement. Could you tell me the price range you have in mind?

E: We would like to increase the price by an additional 5% from the original price. It would be more appealing to us.

H: That is beyond our expectations. We can consider increasing the price by 2%, but we also hope you can provide some other favorable conditions.

E: We can accept a 2% price increase. Additionally, we can offer free after-sales service and include a certain quantity of complimentary items as an extra incentive.

H: That sounds like a good proposal. We also hope to establish a long-term partnership.

E: 您好，我代表我们公司来进行这次商务谈判。我是 A 公司销售部的经理，名叫艾伦。

H: 您好。很高兴见到你。我是黑泽尔。

E: 我们已经收到了您公司的采购价格表，关于产品的种类和数量，我们已经进行了评估。

H: 非常感谢您的反馈。那么，对于我们的价格，请问您有什么看法呢?

E: 你们提出的价格相对于市场来说是比较合理的。但是，我们希望能够有一定的议价空间。

H: 我理解您的想法。我们也希望能够达成一个互利双赢的协议。您能告诉我您希望的价格范围吗?

E: 我们希望能够在原来价格的基础上再增加 5%。这样，对于我们来说会更加有吸引力。

H: 这个幅度有些超出我们的预期。我们可以考虑增加 2% 的价格，但是同时也希望你们能够提供一些其他的优惠条件。

E: 我们可以接受 2% 的增加。同时，我们可以提供免费的售后服务，以及增加一定数量的赠品作为额外的优惠。

H: 这听起来是个不错的提议。我们也希望能够建立长期的合作关系。

Unit 4

合同签订

Contract Signing

谈判达成后，在接下来的合同签订中，英语口语也发挥着重要的作用。通过流利的英语口语，双方能够准确、清晰地表达合同条款和条件，确保双方的权益得到保护。下面就一起来学习一下相关的表达吧。

单词展示

condition [kən'dɪʃn] *n.* 状况

party ['pɑːti] *n.* 当事人

obligation [ˌɒblɪ'geɪʃn] *n.* 义务

legal ['liːgl] *adj.* 法律的

validity [və'lɪdəti] *n.* 有效性

performance [pə'fɔːməns] *n.* 履行

termination [ˌtɜːmɪ'neɪʃn] *n.* 终止

proceed [prə'siːd] *vi.* 继续

breach [briːtʃ] *n.* 违约

liability [ˌlaɪə'bɪləti] *n.* 责任

句子示范

Please confirm the terms and conditions in the contract to make sure there is no ambiguity.

请确认合同中的条款和条件，确保没有任何歧义。

Please read and understand everything in the contract carefully before signing it.

在签署合同之前，请仔细阅读并理解合同的所有内容。

If any term of the contract is breached, liability for breach of contract may arise.

如果违反了合同的任何条款，可能会引发违约责任。

The validity period of the contract is calculated from the date of signing.

合同的有效期限是从签署之日起开始计算。

We need the legal representatives of both parties to sign the contract and affix the official seal.

我们需要双方的法定代表人在合同上签字并加盖公章。

公司A与公司B达成了项目合作，双方分别派出了项目部的经理Jimmy和Leo签订了合作合同。

J=Jimmy　　L=Leo

J: We have drafted and made amendments to the contract, and now we would like to finalize and sign the agreement.

L: Thank you very much for your efforts. We also hope to reach a cooperation agreement as soon as possible. Could you please confirm once again that the terms and conditions in the contract are accurate and correct?

J: I have carefully reviewed the contract to ensure there are no ambiguities. I have also had our legal team review it and confirm its accuracy.

L: Thank you very much for your cooperation. I have read and confirmed the contract in detail. May we proceed with signing the contract?

J: Certainly. I have brought the original and duplicate copies of the contract. After you carefully review the contents, we can proceed with signing.

L: Okay, I have carefully reviewed the contract and have no objections.

J: Please sign and stamp the company seal in the designated places. Then, I will sign and stamp the company seal after you have signed.

L: Okay, please confirm.

J: I have also signed the contract and stamped it with the company seal. The contract is now officially in effect. May we have a successful cooperation.

J: 我们已经进行了合同的起草和修改，现在希望能够最终敲定并签署合同。

L: 非常感谢您的努力。我们也希望能够尽快达成合作协议。请您再次确认合同中的条款和条件是否准确无误。

J: 我已经仔细审核了合同，确保没有任何歧义。我也请了我们的法务团队进行了审查，确认无误。

L: 非常感谢您的配合。我已经对合同进行了详细的阅读和确认。请问我们可以开始签署合同了吗?

J: 当然可以。我已经带来了合同正本和副本，请您仔细核对内容后，我们可以开始签字。

L: 好的，我已经仔细核对过合同内容了，没有异议。

J: 您可以先在相应的位置签字并加盖公司公章。然后，我会在您签署后签字和加盖公司公章。

L: 好的，请您确认。

J: 我也已经在合同上签字并加盖了公司公章。现在，合同正式生效。愿我们合作愉快。

Unit 5

订单支付

Order Payment

订单支付是商务交易的关键步骤，良好的英语口语有助于交易双方就支付事宜进行良好的沟通，并确保支付细节的准确性和安全性。下面来学习一下相关的表达吧。

单词展示

payment [ˈpeɪmənt] *n.* 付款

invoice [ˈɪnvɔɪs] *n.* 发票

transaction [trænˈzækʃn] *n.* 交易

billing [ˈbɪlɪŋ] *n.* 结算

receipt [rɪˈsiːt] *n.* 收据

account [əˈkaʊnt] *n.* 账户

deadline [ˈdedlaɪn] *n.* 截止日期

timely [ˈtaɪmli] *adj.* 及时的

voucher [ˈvaʊtʃə(r)] *n.* 凭证

transfer [ˈtrænsfɜː(r)] *n.* 转账

句子示范

I'd like to make an online payment with my credit card.

我想使用信用卡进行在线支付。

Please provide your bank account information for a bank transfer payment.

请提供您的银行账户信息，以便我们进行转账支付。

Please note that the payment for the order must be completed within two business days.

请注意，订单需在两个工作日内完成付款。

If you choose cash on delivery, you can make the payment upon receiving the goods.

如果您选择货到付款，您可以在收到商品后进行支付。

A 公司的销售经理 Mandy 与 B 公司的 Peter 通话，确认订单支付相关内容。

M=Mandy　　P=Peter

M: Hello, Peter, I'm Mandy, the sales manager of Company A. We have recently received an order from your company, and I would like to confirm the payment details with you.

P: Okay.

M: First of all, may I ask which payment method you would like to use?

P: We usually prefer bank transfer for payment. Please provide us with your company's bank account information so that we can proceed with the transfer.

M: Alright.

P: We will arrange the bank transfer payment as soon as possible. Also, is there a payment deadline we should be aware of?

M: Yes, we usually require the payment to be completed within three business days after order confirmation. This will allow us to arrange timely delivery.

P: Understood. We will make the payment promptly to ensure on-time delivery of the order.

M: Thank you very much. Additionally, once the payment is completed, please send us the payment voucher for our verification and confirmation.

P: No problem. We will send you the payment voucher for your confirmation.

M: Thank you for your cooperation. We look forward to a fruitful collaboration.

M: 你好，彼得，我是曼迪，A公司的销售经理。我们最近收到了您公司的订单，我想和您确认一下支付相关的事宜。

P: 好的。

M: 首先，请问您打算使用哪种支付方式？

P: 我们公司通常使用银行转账进行支付。请提供您公司的银行账户信息，以便我们完成转账。

M: 好的。

P: 我们将尽快安排转账支付。另外，请问是否有支付截止日期？

M: 是的，我们通常要求在订单确认后的三个工作日内完成支付。这样我们就能及时安排发货。

P: 明白了。我们会尽快完成支付，以确保订单按时发货。

M: 非常感谢。还有一件事，一旦支付完成，请您将支付凭证发送给我们，以便我们核对并确认。

P: 没问题，我们会将支付凭证发送给您进行确认。

M: 非常感谢您的合作。期待我们合作愉快。

Unit 6

货物运输

Cargo Delivery

运用流利的英语口语，能够与承运商、客户进行有效的沟通，确保货物运输的顺利进行。下面让我们一起来学习一下相关的表达吧。

单词展示

cargo [ˈkɑːɡəʊ] *n.* 货物

carrier [ˈkæriə(r)] *n.* 承运人

container [kənˈteɪnə(r)] *n.* 集装箱

import [ˈɪmpɔːt] *v./n.* 进口

export [ˈekspɔːt] *v./n.* 出口

customs [ˈkʌstəmz] *n.* 海关

port [pɔːt] *n.* 港口

route [ruːt] *n.* 路线，航线

appropriate [əˈprəʊpriət] *adj.* 适当的

integrity [ɪnˈteɡrəti] *n.* 完整

句子示范

We need to track the shipment of goods to ensure that we can keep abreast of the location and status of the goods.

我们需要跟踪货物的运输情况，以确保能够及时了解货物的位置和状态。

Please provide a detailed plan for the loading and unloading of the goods to ensure the smooth progress of the transportation.

请提供货物的装载和卸载的详细计划，以确保运输的顺利进行。

Before the goods are delivered, we need to confirm that all documents and supporting documents are complete and accurate.

在货物交付之前，我们需要确认所有的文件和证明文件是否完整和准确。

We hope that the goods can pass through customs smoothly and all import and export procedures will be completed on time.

我们希望货物能够顺利通过海关，并按时完成所有的进出口手续。

A公司与B公司达成项目合作后，A公司的销售部经理Sandy与B公司的经理Roy确认物流信息。

S=Sandy　　R=Roy

S: Hello, Roy. I would like to confirm the logistics and transportation of our goods. When do you plan to arrange for the shipment?

R: Okay, we will arrange for the shipment of the order as soon as possible. Based on our logistics plan, we estimate that the order will be delivered to your warehouse next Wednesday.

S: Thank you very much. Additionally, we would like to receive a delivery notification before the goods are delivered, so that we can make timely arrangements for receiving and inspection.

R: We will notify you in advance of the arrival time of the goods to ensure that you can make necessary preparations for receiving.

S: We also want to ensure the safety of the goods during transportation.

R: We place great importance on the packaging and protection of the goods. We will use appropriate packaging materials and methods to ensure that the goods are not damaged during transportation.

S: If there is any damage or loss to the order during transportation, we hope to receive corresponding compensation and solutions.

R: We will make every effort to ensure the safety and integrity of the order. In the unfortunate event of damage or loss, we will provide compensation and solutions in accordance with the terms and conditions of the contract.

S: Okay.

R: If you have any other questions regarding the delivery of the order, feel free to contact me at any time.

S: 你好，罗伊，我想和你确认一下我们货物的物流运输，你们打算什么时候安排发货呢？

R: 好的，我们会尽快安排订单的发货。根据我们的物流计划，预计订单将在下周三送达您的仓库。

S: 非常感谢。另外，我们希望在货物交付前能够收到一个交付通知，这样我们可以及时安排接收和验收。

R: 我们会提前通知您货物的到达时间，以确保您能够及时做好接收的准备工作。

S: 我们还希望确保货物在运输过程中的安全。

R: 我们非常注重货物的包装和保护。我们会使用适当的包装材料和方式，以确保货物在运输过程中不受损坏。

S: 如果订单在运输过程中有任何损坏或遗失，我们希望能够得到相应的赔偿和解决方案。

R: 我们会尽一切努力确保订单的安全和完整。如果不幸发生损坏或遗失，我们会根据合同中的条款和条件进行相应的赔偿和解决。

S: 好的。

R: 如果还有其他关于订单交付的问题，随时与我联系。

Chapter 2 新媒体运营

在当今数字化时代，新媒体运营已经成为一种重要的宣传和推广手段。新媒体运营是指在互联网和社交媒体平台上使用各种策略和技巧，以推广品牌、建立在线社区和吸引受众的过程。而对于新媒体运营者来讲，如果能用流利的英语口语清晰地表达思想和观点，将会让自己的自媒体运营之路走得更远更广。所以，学习新媒体运营领域的相关英语表达很有必要。

Unit 1

文案撰写

Copy Writing

新媒体运营离不开准确、生动的文案，所以文案撰写是不可或缺的一个环节。那么，与文案撰写相关的英语表达，你知道多少呢？下面一起来学习一下吧。

单词展示

content [ˈkɒntent] *n.* 内容

headline [ˈhedlaɪn] *n.* 标题

introduction [ˌɪntrəˈdʌkʃn] *n.* 引言

body [ˈbɒdi] *n.* 正文，主体

proofread [ˈpruːfriːd] *v.* 校对

edit [ˈedɪt] *v.* 编辑

format [ˈfɔːmæt] *v.* 格式化

tone [təʊn] *n.* 语气，口吻

audience [ˈɔːdiəns] *n.* 观众

research [rɪˈsɜːtʃ] *v.* 研究

句子示范

To increase click-through rates, you need a captivating headline.

你需要写一个引人注目的标题，这样才能提升点击率。

We need to highlight the unique selling points of the product to pique the interest of potential customers.

我们需要突出产品的独特卖点，以激发潜在客户的兴趣。

Conduct thorough market research and competitive analysis before crafting the copy.

在撰写文案之前，请进行充分的市场调研和竞争对比分析。

We need to regularly review and update the copy to adapt to market changes and demands.

我们需要定期审查和更新文案，以适应市场的变化和需求。

We will customize the copy according to your needs, so please provide us with the tone of your product.

我们会根据您的需求来定制文案，希望您能够给我们提供您产品的调性。

Sidney是A公司的产品经理，想要给产品做推广运营，找到了C公司的新媒体文案编辑Anna，二人对此进行了商讨。

S=Sidney A=Anna

S: Hello, I am the Marketing Manager of Company A. We need help in writing some copy related to new media operations. I was wondering if you could assist us.

A: I would be happy to help. Can you please specify the particular aspect of new media operations that the copy is for?

S: We need some copy for social media advertising that can capture the attention of our target audience and encourage them to engage with us.

A: Understood. First, please provide some information about your target audience, such as age, gender, and interests. This will help us better tailor the style and language of the copy.

S: Our target audience is mainly young people aged between 18 and 35, with a high interest in fashion, technology, and health.

A: Great, I will write the copy based on this information. What tone do you prefer for the copy? Would you like it to be humorous or more serious?

S: We would like the copy to have a humorous and light-hearted tone, while still maintaining a professional and engaging quality.

A: I will incorporate some humorous elements into the copy while ensuring that the message is effectively conveyed and goals are achieved.

S: We need to regularly review and update the copy to adapt to changes in the new media landscape and audience demands.

A: Yes, the new media landscape changes rapidly. We will closely monitor market trends and promptly optimize and update the copy as needed.

S: 你好，我是 A 公司的市场营销经理。我们最近需要撰写一些与新媒体运营有关的文案，我想请你帮忙。

A: 很高兴能为您提供帮助。请问具体是哪方面的新媒体运营文案呢?

S: 我们需要一些关于社交媒体广告的文案，能够吸引目标受众的注意力并促使他们与我们互动。

A: 明白了。首先，请提供一些关于目标受众的信息，比如年龄、性别、兴趣爱好等，这样我们能够更好地定位文案的风格和语言。

S: 我们的目标受众主要是年轻人，年龄在 18 到 35 岁之间，对时尚、科技和健康有较高的关注度。

A: 好的，我会根据这些信息来撰写文案。请问您希望文案的调性是什么样的？是幽默风趣还是严肃正经？

S: 我们希望文案能够有一些幽默和轻松的调性，但同时也要保持专业和吸引人的特点。

A: 我会在文案中运用一些幽默的元素，同时确保不会影响信息的传递和目标的实现。

S: 我们需要定期审查和更新文案，以适应新媒体环境和受众需求的变化。

A: 是的，新媒体环境变化迅速，我们会密切关注市场动态，并及时进行文案的优化和更新。

Unit 2

活动策划

Program Planning

活动策划是新媒体运营的重要组成部分，与之相关的英语表达十分丰富，掌握了相关的英语表达，可以更好地进行活动策划。下面就一起来学习一下与活动策划相关的英语表达吧。

单词展示

venue [ˈvenjuː] *n.* 场地，会场

budget [ˈbʌdʒɪt] *n.* 预算

promotion [prəˈməʊʃn] *n.* 推广，宣传

marketing [ˈmɑːkɪtɪŋ] *n.* 市场营销

sponsorship [ˈspɒnsəʃɪp] *n.* 赞助

program [ˈprəʊɡræm] *n.* 程序，节目

identity [aɪˈdentəti] *n.* 身份

media [ˈmiːdiə] *n.* 媒体

entertainment [ˌentəˈteɪnmənt] *n.* 娱乐，文娱节目

decoration [ˌdekəˈreɪʃn] *n.* 装饰，装潢

句子示范

We need to determine the time, venue, and format of the new media event to ensure its smooth execution.

我们需要确定新媒体活动的时间、地点和形式，以确保活动的顺利进行。

We need to design a unique new media event to enhance brand awareness and recognition.

我们需要设计一个独特的新媒体活动，以提升品牌的知名度和认可度。

Ensure the event information is widely disseminated on social media platforms to attract more audience attention and participation.

确保活动信息在社交媒体上得到广泛传播，吸引更多的受众关注和参与。

Please assist in developing a detailed promotional plan, including social media advertising, to expand the event's impact.

请帮忙制订一份详细的推广计划，包括社交媒体宣传等，以扩大活动的影响力。

B 公司要举办一次新媒体活动，经理 Tim 与策划部员工 Ada 和 Sandy 一起开会商讨活动策划方案。

T=Tim　　A=Ada　　S=Sandy

T: Today, we're going to discuss a new task for planning a new media event. We aim to enhance our brand awareness and user engagement through this new media event.

A: Specifically, what new media platforms and content formats should we consider?

T: We want to make full use of social media platforms such as Weibo, WeChat, TikTok, as well as online interactive activities like live streaming and topic discussions.

S: What are the specific roles and responsibilities for this task?

T: Ada, you will be in charge of developing the promotion plan and contacting partners, including social media promotion. Sandy, you will be responsible for designing the visual identity and copy for the event.

A: Okay, I will create a detailed promotion plan.

S: I will design a unique visual identity and copy to enhance the attractiveness and dissemination of the event.

T: Additionally, we need to ensure the technical equipment and on-site setup for the event. I will contact relevant suppliers and venues to ensure everything is ready.

A: We also need to consider interactive activities and offline communication during the event. I will discuss with Sandy to ensure interactivity and engagement at the event venue.

T: Excellent, I will organize regular meetings to ensure the progress and promptly address any issues.

T: 今天我们要讨论的是一个新的新媒体活动策划任务。我们希望通过这次新媒体活动来提升我们品牌的知名度和用户互动性。

A: 具体来说，我们要考虑哪些新媒体平台和内容形式呢?

T: 我们希望能够充分利用社交媒体平台，比如微博、微信和抖音，以及线上互动活动，比如直播和话题讨论。

S: 那么具体的任务分工是什么呢?

T: 艾达，你负责制订推广计划和联系合作伙伴，包括社交媒体宣传。桑迪，你负责设计活动的视觉形象和文案。

A: 好的，我会制订一个详细的推广计划。

S: 我会设计一套独特的视觉形象和文案，以提升活动的吸引力和传播效果。

T: 另外，我们还需要确保活动的技术设备和现场布置。我会联系相关的供应商和场地，保证一切准备就绪。

A: 我们还需要考虑活动的互动环节和线下交流。我会和桑迪商讨，确保活动现场的互动性和参与度。

T: 非常好，我会定期组织会议，确保活动进展顺利，并及时解决问题。

Unit 3

图文排版

Picture & Text Layout

图文排版就是将文字、图片、图形等元素进行合理排版布局的过程。与新媒体运营中图文排版相关的英语表达你知道多少呢？了解与之相关的英语表达，可以让工作更加顺利。下面就来具体学习一下吧。

单词展示

typography [taɪˈpɒgrəfi] *n.* 排字，印刷术

layout [ˈleɪaʊt] *n.* 布局，版面设计

alignment [əˈlaɪnmənt] *n.* 对齐，排列

hierarchy [ˈhaɪərɑːki] *n.* 层次，等级制度

font [fɒnt] *n.* 字体，字形

tracking [ˈtrækɪŋ] *n.* 字间距，字体间距调整

grid [grɪd] *n.* 网格，格子

margin [ˈmɑːdʒɪn] *n.* 页边距，边缘

column [ˈkɒləm] *n.* 栏目，列

overcrowd [ˌəuvəˈkraʊd] *n.* 过度拥挤

句子示范

Ensure that the size and position of each text box adhere to the design specifications to maintain overall consistency.

请确保每个文本框的尺寸和位置都符合设计规范，以保持整体的一致性。

Leave sufficient white space in the design to avoid overcrowding between text and images.

在设计中要留出足够的空白区域，以避免文字和图像之间的拥挤。

We aim to facilitate reader comprehension and retention through visual layout and typography.

我们希望通过图文排版的方式，让读者更容易理解和记忆内容。

Pay attention to letter spacing in the design to ensure overall balance and aesthetics of the text.

在设计中要注意字母之间的距离，以确保文字的整体平衡和美观。

Please place this headline in the center of the page to highlight its importance.

请将这个标题放在页面的中心位置，以突出重点。

A 公司的 Linda 认为宣传页还有些不理想，便向 C 公司的排版人员 Fiona 提出了一些要求。

L=Linda　　F=Fiona

L: Hello! I'm Linda from Company A. The promotional page we have recently designed is still somewhat unsatisfactory. I have some suggestions and requests that I would like to discuss with you.

F: I will do my best to meet your requirements. Please let me know which aspects of the flyer you are unsatisfied with.

L: First, I feel that we need to make adjustments to the spacing between text and images. The current layout makes the text and images feel too crowded, giving off a cramped vibe. I would like to increase the spacing between them to make the entire layout look more clean and refreshing.

F: Understood.

L: Additionally, I have some requests regarding the font colors. The current color contrast between the font and background is not sufficient, making the text less prominent. I would like to choose brighter and more vibrant font colors to make the text stand out.

F: Alright, do you have any specific color preferences?

L: I would like the font colors to align with our company's brand image. Our brand color is blue, so I suggest selecting bright colors that go well with blue, such as vibrant yellow or bright green.

F: Understood, I will do my best to meet your requests.

L: 你好！我是 A 公司的琳达，我们最近设计的宣传页还有些不理想，我想向你提出一些建议和要求。

F: 我会尽力满足你的要求。请告诉我你对宣传页的哪些方面感到不满意。

L: 首先，在文字和图像之间的距离上，我觉得需要进行调整。目前的排版让文字和图像显得过于拥挤，给人一种拥堵的感觉。我希望能够增加它们之间的距离，使整个版面更加清爽。

F: 明白了。

L: 另外，我对字体颜色也有一些要求。现在的宣传页中使用的字体颜色和背景颜色对比度不够，导致文字不够醒目。我希望能够选择更加明亮和鲜艳的字体颜色，使文字更加突出。

F: 好的，你有什么具体的颜色偏好吗？

L: 我希望字体颜色能够与我们公司的品牌形象相符，我们的标志色是蓝色，所以我建议选择与蓝色搭配良好的亮色，比如鲜黄或明绿等。

F: 明白了，我会尽力满足你的要求。

Unit 4

视频剪辑

Video Editing

视频剪辑是将视频片段、音频和图像有机地组合在一起，创造出令人赏心悦目的视觉作品。掌握与视频剪辑相关的英语表达益处多多，下面一起来学习吧。

单词展示

footage [ˈfʊtɪdʒ] *n.* 录像素材，片段

clip [klɪp] *n.* 剪辑，片段

cut [kʌt] *n.* 剪辑，剪切

trim [trɪm] *v.* 修剪，削减

overlay [ˌəʊvəˈleɪ] *v.* 叠加，覆盖

effect [ɪˈfekt] *n.* 效果，影响

timeline [ˈtaɪmlaɪn] *n.* 时间轴，时间线

rendering [ˈrendərɪŋ] *n.* 渲染，呈现

montage [ˌmɒnˈtɑːʒ] *n.* 蒙太奇，剪辑组合

soundtrack [ˈsaʊndtræk] *n.* 配乐，音轨

句子示范

We need to trim the video to remove irrelevant parts while maintaining content coherence.

我们需要对视频进行裁剪，去除无关的部分，以保持内容的连贯性。

Montage effects in video editing can combine multiple shots or scenes to create new visual effects.

视频剪辑中的蒙太奇效果可以将多个镜头或画面组合在一起，创造出新的视觉效果。

Arrange video footage on the timeline to control the pacing and narrative flow of the video.

在时间轴上安排视频素材，以控制视频的节奏和故事流程。

After completing the video editing, render the video and export a high-quality final video file.

完成视频剪辑后，请进行渲染并导出高质量的最终视频文件。

I need to edit these video clips to create an engaging video.

我需要将这些视频素材进行剪辑，以制作出一个有吸引力的视频。

Tim 接到了一个视频剪辑的任务，但他有些地方不清楚，便向 Fiona 求助。

T=Tim　　F=Fiona

T: Fiona, I know you’re a talented video editor, and I need your help with a project.

F: Of course, how can I assist you?

T: It’s a promotional video for a company, and we need an attractive and professional edited version. I’ve gathered some footage, but I’m not sure how to achieve the desired effect.

F: Firstly, in the editing process, ensure the video has smooth transitions and coherence. Consider adding some transitional effects to enhance the viewing experience.

T: Understood.

F: The video should also have an impressive opening and a clear ending. Pay attention to the overall pacing and storytelling during the editing process.

T: Okay.

F: Additionally, please ensure the selection of soundtracks and background music aligns with the video content to enhance the audience's viewing experience.

T: I'll carefully choose suitable soundtracks and background music.

F: I will organize a detailed list of precautions for you to help you better edit videos. I am looking forward to seeing the final edited version.

T: 菲奥娜，我知道你是一个很擅长视频剪辑的人才，我有一个项目需要你的帮助。

F: 当然可以，需要我怎么帮助你？

T: 这是一个公司的推广视频，我们需要一个有吸引力且专业的剪辑版本。我已经收集了一些素材，但我不知道怎么剪辑出好的效果。

F: 首先，在剪辑过程中，要确保视频的流畅性和连贯性，并考虑添加一些过渡效果以增强观看体验。

T: 明白。

F: 视频还要有一个令人印象深刻的开头，以及一个清晰的结尾。在剪辑过程中，要注意整体节奏和故事的表达。

T: 好的。

F: 另外，请确保音轨和背景音乐的选择与视频内容相匹配，以增强观众的观看体验。

T: 我会仔细挑选适合的音轨和背景音乐。

F: 我会给你整理一份详细的注意事项，帮助你更好地剪辑视频。我很期待看到最终的剪辑版本。

Unit 5

视频发布

Video Posting

视频剪辑完成之后，接下来就是视频发布了。与视频发布相关的口语表达你知道多少呢？下面一起来学习一下吧。

单词 展示

upload [ˌʌpˈləʊd] *v.* 上传，上载	publish [ˈpʌblɪʃ] *v.* 发布，公开
share [ʃeə(r)] *v.* 分享，共享	elements [ˈelɪmənts] *n.* 元素
platform [ˈplætfɔːm] *n.* 平台，载体	subscriber [səbˈskraɪbə(r)] *n.* 订阅者，用户
visual [ˈvɪʒʊəl] *adj.* 视觉的	caption [ˈkæpʃn] *n.* 字幕，标题
comment [ˈkɒment] *n.* 评论，留言	channel [ˈtʃænl] *n.* 频道，渠道

句子示范

We plan to release this new video tomorrow to attract a larger audience.

我们计划在明天发布这个新视频，以吸引更多的观众。

Before releasing the video, please ensure that its quality and content meet our requirements.

在发布视频之前，请确保它的质量和内容都符合我们的要求。

After releasing the video, please respond promptly to audience comments and feedback to foster better engagement.

在发布视频之后，请及时回复观众的评论和反馈，以建立更好的互动。

Use analytic tools to track audience preferences and behaviors after the video's release, optimizing our video content.

在发布视频之后，请使用分析工具来跟踪观众的喜好和行为，以优化我们的视频内容。

Through collaborations and cross-platform promotion, we can expand the video's viewership and increase its exposure.

通过合作与跨平台推广，我们可以扩大视频的观众群体并增加其曝光率。

Cindy 是刚入职的新员工，发布视频之前，总监 Peter 提醒她，发布视频前要注意的地方。

C=Cindy P=Peter

P: Hi Cindy! I have some precautions to tell you about video publishing.

C: Okay.

P: First, before publishing a video, make sure that its quality and content meet our requirements. Check the video's visual and audio quality, as well as elements like text and images.

C: Okay, are there any other things to pay attention to?

P: Yes, the cover design is crucial. An eye-catching cover can attract more clicks and views. Consider using beautiful images and compelling titles to design the cover.

C: Okay, I'll pay attention to the cover design to make sure it grabs the audience's attention.

P: After publishing the video, be sure to promptly respond to audience comments and feedback. This helps foster engagement and shows that we value and care about our audience.

C: I understand.

P: You go ahead and double-check the video, and once I've reviewed it, you can proceed with publishing it.

C: Okay, got it. I will carefully review it.

P: 嗨，辛迪！关于视频发布，我还有一些注意事项要告诉你。

C: 好的。

P: 首先，发布视频之前，请确保视频的质量和内容都符合我们的要求。要仔细检查视频的画质、音质以及文字、图像等元素。

C: 好的，还有其他需要注意的地方吗？

P: 是的，封面设计是很重要的一点。一个吸引人的封面能够吸引更多的点击和观看。请考虑使用精美的图片和吸引人的标题来设计封面。

C: 好的，我会注意封面的设计，确保它能够吸引观众的注意。

P: 发布视频后，请及时回复观众的评论和反馈。这有助于建立良好的互动，并表明我们对观众的关注和重视。

C: 明白。

P: 你先检查一遍视频，然后做好视频发布的前期工作，我检查后，你再发布这个视频。

C: 好的，我会仔细检查的。

Unit 6

数据分析

Data Analysis

数据分析是通过收集、处理和解读数据来获取有价值的洞见和决策支持的过程。与数据分析相关的英语表达具体如下，我们一起来学习一下吧。

单词展示

insight [ˈɪnsaɪt] *n.* 洞察，深刻见解

interpretation [ɪnˌtɜːprəˈteɪʃn] *n.* 解释

statistics [stəˈtɪstɪks] *n.* 统计数据，统计学

revenue [ˈrevənjuː] *n.* 收入，营收

metrics [ˈmetrɪks] *n.* 指标，度量标准

rate [reɪt] *n.* 比率，速率

trend [trend] *n.* 趋势，潮流

engagement [ɪnˈɡeɪdʒmənt] *n.* 参与度

viewership [ˈvjuːəʃɪp] *n.* 观众人数，收视率

popular [ˈpɒpjələ(r)] *adj.* 流行的

句子示范

Video data analysis can help us identify the most popular video content and platforms.

视频数据分析可以帮助我们确定最受欢迎的视频内容和平台。

By observing video click-through rates and playback duration, we can assess audience interest and engagement.

通过观察视频的点击率和播放时长，我们可以评估观众的兴趣和参与度。

We need to use professional data analytic tools to collect, organize, and interpret video data.

我们需要使用专业的数据分析工具来收集、整理和解读视频数据。

We need to conduct video data analysis to understand audience preferences and behaviors.

我们需要进行视频数据分析，以了解观众的喜好和行为。

Roland 就视频发布后的数据与员工 Vincent 和 Tony 开会，商讨以后的注意事项。

R=Roland　　V=Vincent　　T=Tony

R: Today, I'd like to discuss the data analysis results of the new media videos we recently released.

V: We put a lot of time and effort into creating these videos, hoping to gain valuable insights.

R: Absolutely. First, let's look at the data on audience watch time and views. According to the analysis results, we found that two videos had longer watch times and relatively higher view counts. This indicates that our investment in these two videos has had a positive effect.

T: So, do these two videos have anything in common?

R: We can further analyze audience feedback, such as the number of likes, comments, and shares. By observing this data, we can see that the audience is more engaged with these two videos, which may be attributed to the attractiveness and interactivity of the video content.

V: Can we draw inspiration from these successful videos for future video production?

R: Definitely. Based on the data analysis results, we can identify which types of content and styles the audience prefers, and then apply these elements in our future video production. This will help improve audience engagement and view counts.

T: In addition to watch time and interaction data, we can also focus on video conversion rates and user behavior, which will provide important insights for our marketing and promotion strategies.

R: To summarize, we need to comprehensively analyze various aspects of data, including watch time, interaction data, conversion rates, user behavior, and social media performance, to obtain a more comprehensive understanding of video data analysis results.

R: 今天我想和大家一起讨论一下我们最近发布的新媒体视频的数据分析结果。

V: 我们花了很多时间和精力制作这些视频，希望能得到一些有价值的信息。

R: 没错。首先，让我们来看一下观众观看时间和观看量的数据。根据分析结果，我们发现有两个视频的观看时间较长，观看量也相对较高。这意味着我们在这两个视频上的投入产生了积极的效果。

T: 那么，这两个视频有什么共同点吗？

R: 我们可以进一步分析观众的反馈，如喜欢和评论的数量，以及分享率。通过观察这些数据，我们可以看出观众对这两个视频的互动程度更高，这可能与视频内容的吸引力和互动性有关。

V: 那么我们是否可以从这些成功的视频中汲取灵感，用于未来的视频制作?

R: 当然。根据数据分析的结果，我们可以确定观众喜欢哪些类型的内容和风格，然后在今后的视频制作中应用这些元素。这将有助于提高我们的观众参与度和观看量。

T: 除了观看时间和互动数据，我们还可以关注视频的转化率和用户行为，这将对我们的营销和推广策略有重要的启示。

R: 总结一下，我们需要综合分析观看时间、互动数据、转化率、用户行为以及社交媒体表现等多个方面的数据，以获取更全面的视频数据分析结果。

Chapter 3 快递物流

现在的快递物流行业逐步向国际化发展，需要与全球供应链伙伴、客户和运输人员进行有效的沟通，而英语在这个过程中发挥着关键作用。英语口语对于保持顺畅的沟通、解决问题和促进国际合作至关重要，也为快递物流行业的发展和全球业务提供了关键支持。

Unit 1

揽收包裹

Receiving Parcel

揽收包裹是快递物流行业的重要环节，需要快递员与寄件人进行有效的沟通和协调。下面就一起来学习揽收包裹过程中常用到的英语表达吧。

单词展示

collection [kəˈlekʃn] *n.* 收集，集合

pickup [ˈpɪkʌp] *n.* 取件，接送

receipt [rɪˈsiːt] *n.* 收据，收条

courier [ˈkʊriə(r)] *n.* 信使，快递员

doorstep [ˈdɔːstep] *n.* 门前

convenient [kənˈviːniənt] *adj.* 方便的

inquire [ɪnˈkwaɪə(r)] *v.* 询问

express [ɪkˈspres] *adj.* 快递的，迅速的

postage [ˈpəʊstɪdʒ] *n.* 邮费

reservation [ˌrezəˈveɪʃn] *n.* 预订，预约

句子示范

The collector will come to your door to collect your package within the designated time.

揽收员会在指定时间内上门收取您的包裹。

Please ensure that the package is properly packaged when it is collected.

揽收包裹时，请确保包裹已妥善包装。

You can hand over the package to the staff at the designated collection point.

您可以在指定的揽收点将包裹交给工作人员。

During the collection process, please make sure that the package label is clear and readable.

揽收过程中，请确保包裹标签清晰可读。

We provide free doorstep collection service.

我们提供免费的上门揽收服务。

Amy 想要寄一个快递，便打电话咨询 C 快递公司的服务人员 Cindy 有关上门揽收包裹的问题。

A=Amy　　C=Cindy

A: Hello, I'd like to inquire about parcel collection.

C: Certainly, I'm happy to assist you. What specific information would you like to know?

A: I have some important goods that need to be shipped, but due to time constraints, I would like to arrange for a doorstep pickup.

C: No problem, we provide doorstep collection service. Could you please provide me with your address and a convenient time frame? We will arrange for a dedicated personnel to come and collect the parcel.

A: That's great! I'm in Zone A, and tomorrow between 2 PM and 5 PM would be convenient for me.

C: Alright, I have made a note of that. Could you please provide an approximate weight and dimensions of your package so that we can arrange an appropriate transport vehicle?

A: The weight should be around 5 kilograms, and the dimensions are approximately 40 centimeters in length, 30 centimeters in width, and 20 centimeters in height.

C: Understood. We will arrange a suitable transport vehicle to collect your package. Also, please ensure that the package is properly packaged to prevent any damage during transportation.

A: Okay, I will pay special attention to the packaging.

C: We will provide you with a collection confirmation form. You just need to sign it upon collection. Please prepare the necessary sender and recipient information, which we will fill out on the collection form.

A: I see.

C: Thank you very much for your support and recommendation! Wishing you a smooth delivery, and feel free to contact us if you need any further assistance.

A: 您好，我想咨询一下关于揽收包裹的事宜。

C: 当然，很高兴为您解答。请问您需要了解哪方面的信息？

A: 我有一些重要货物需要寄送，但是由于时间紧迫，我希望能够安排上门揽收。

C: 没问题，我们提供上门揽收服务。您可以告诉我您所在的地址和方便的时间段，我们会派专人前往揽收。

A: 太好了！我在 A 区，明天下午 2 点到 5 点之间比较方便。

C: 好的，我已经记录下来了。请问您的包裹大致有多重和多大尺寸，以便我们安排合适的运输工具。

A: 大致重量应该在 5 公斤左右，尺寸是 40 厘米长、30 厘米宽、20 厘米高。

C: 明白了。我们将会安排适合的运输工具来揽收您的包裹。另外，请您确保包裹已经妥善包装，以防在运输过程中发生损坏。

A: 好的，我会特别注意包装。

C: 我们会为您提供揽收确认单，您只需在揽收时签署即可。同时，请您准备好相应的寄件人和收件人信息，我们将填写在揽收单上。

A: 明白了。

C: 非常感谢您的支持和推荐！祝您寄送顺利，如果有任何需要，请随时联系我们。

Unit 2

分拣包裹

Parcel Sorting

分拣包裹是快递物流中的重要环节，与之相关的英语表达非常多。下面列举了一些与分拣包裹相关的英语表达，一起来学习一下吧。

单词展示

barcode [ˈbɑːrkəʊd] *n.* 条形码

label [ˈleɪbl] *n.* 标签

scan [skæn] *v.* 扫描

destination [ˌdestɪˈneɪʃn] *n.* 目的地

handling [ˈhændlɪŋ] *n.* 处理

picking [ˈpɪkɪŋ] *n.* 拣选

center [ˈsentə(r)] *n.* 中心

automated [ˈɔːtəmeɪtɪd] *adj.* 自动化的

conveyor [kənˈveɪə(r)] *n.* 传送带

ensure [ɪnˈʃʊə(r)] *v.* 确保

句子示范

We are sorting the packages to ensure accurate delivery to the destination.

我们正在分拣包裹，以便准确送达目的地。

During the sorting process, each package needs to be handled and selected carefully.

分拣过程中，需要仔细处理和挑选每个包裹。

You can track the sorting and transportation process of the packages through a tracking number.

你可以通过追踪号码来跟踪包裹的分拣和运送过程。

Automated sorting systems can improve the efficiency and accuracy of package sorting.

自动化分拣系统能够提高包裹分拣的效率和准确性。

Scott 刚入职快递公司，负责分拣快递部分，他向老员工 Toby 询问如何分拣包裹。

S=Scott　　T=Toby

S: Hello, I am a new employee. I heard you have been working here for a long time. Can you teach me some skills?

T: Of course! Welcome to our team. Firstly, you need to familiarize yourself with the sorting system we use.

S: Great.

T: We use barcode scanners to scan the barcodes on each package. The system will automatically recognize the destination and sorting information. Make sure you remain stable while scanning to accurately read the barcodes.

S: Understood.

T: After scanning, the system will assign the packages to different sorting zones. You need to ensure that you place the packages in the correct zones to ensure they are handled correctly.

S: It sounds a bit complicated. How do I determine the correct sorting zones?

T: We have instructional labels or color codes indicating each zone. Make sure you carefully read the labels on each package and place them in the respective zones.

S: Okay, I'll read and follow the label instructions carefully. Are there any other tips to improve my sorting efficiency?

T: Absolutely! One important tip is to pay close attention to the markings and features on each package to quickly identify the destination. Additionally, keeping your workspace clean and organized can help you find the required packages faster.

S: Thank you very much for your guidance and advice! I'll strive to stay calm, focused, and accurate.

S: 你好，我是新来的员工，听说你在这里工作很久了，能教授我一些技能吗？

T: 当然可以！欢迎加入我们的团队。首先，你需要了解我们使用的分拣系统。

S: 好的。

T: 我们使用条形码扫描仪来扫描每个包裹上的条形码。系统会自动识别目的地和排序信息。确保你在扫描时保持稳定，以便准确读取条形码。

S: 明白了。

T: 在扫描完成后，系统会将包裹分配到不同的分拣区域。你需要注意将包裹放置在正确的区域中，以确保它们被正确处理。

S: 这听起来有些复杂，如何确定正确的分拣区域呢？

T: 我们会有指示标签或颜色代码，用于指示每个区域。确保你仔细阅读每个包裹上的标签，并将其放置在相应的区域中。

S: 好的，我会认真阅读和遵循标签指示。还有其他技巧可以提高我的分拣效率吗？

T: 当然！一个重要的技巧是，仔细观察每个包裹上的标记和特征，以便快速识别目的地。此外，保持工作区整洁和有序，这样可以帮助你更快地找到所需的包裹。

S: 非常感谢你的指导和建议！我会努力做到冷静、专注和准确。

Unit 3

转运包裹

Parcel Transhipment

转运包裹是指将包裹从一个运输节点转移到另一个节点，通常涉及各种交流。在这个过程中，良好的英语口语交流能力至关重要。下面让我们一起学习一下吧。

单词展示

return [rɪˈtɜːn] *n.* 返回	transportation [ˌtrænspɔːˈteɪʃn] *n.* 运输
transfer [ˈtrænsfɜː(r)] *v.* 转移	chain [tʃeɪn] *n.* 链条
haulage [ˈhɔːlɪdʒ] *n.* 运输	transshipment [trænsˈʃɪpmənt] *n.* 转运
forwarding [ˈfɔːwədɪŋ] *n.* 转发	awaiting [əˈweɪtɪŋ] *adj.* 等待中的
status [ˈsteɪtəs] *n.* 状态	record [ˈrekɔːd] *n.* 记录

句子示范

The forwarding company is responsible for transporting the packages from the warehouse to the destination.

转运公司会负责将包裹从仓库送到目的地。

Please ensure that the package labels are clear and visible for tracking during the forwarding process.

请确保包裹的标签清晰可见，以便在转运过程中进行跟踪。

If you have any questions or concerns, please contact the customer service department of the forwarding company promptly.

若有任何问题或疑虑，请及时联系转运公司的客服部门。

I need to provide detailed information about the packages to the forwarding company.

我需要提供包裹的详细信息给转运公司。

The forwarding fees for the packages will be calculated based on their weight and distance.

包裹的转运费用将根据重量和距离进行计算。

Benny 查不到自己的快递信息，打电话给快递中心工作人员 Henry 帮忙查询。

B=Benny H=Henry

B: Hello, I've been unable to track the status of my recent package, so I'd like to inquire about it.

H: Hello, I can assist you with that. Could you please provide me with the tracking number of your package?

B: The tracking number is ABC123456789.

H: Alright, let me check that for you. Please wait a moment.

(*A few minutes later*)

H: Thank you for your patience. According to our records, your package has arrived at our transit center and is awaiting further transportation.

B: Transit center? What does that mean?

H: A transit center is a hub used for transferring packages from the origin to the destination. During this stage, the package may need to wait until there is sufficient volume for transportation.

B: When will I be able to know the latest status of my package?

H: Generally, we update the package's status once it reaches the transit center. You can check the status anytime using the tracking number or wait for us to send you the latest tracking information.

B: Alright.

H: We will provide you with the latest tracking information as soon as possible. If you have any other questions or need assistance, feel free to contact our customer service department.

B: 喂，你好！我的包裹最近一直没有更新快递信息，我想查一下它的状态。

H: 你好，我可以帮你查询。请问你有包裹的快递单号吗？

B: 单号是 ABC123456789。

H: 好的，让我查一下。稍等片刻。

（几分钟后）

H: 感谢你的耐心等待。根据我们的记录，你的包裹目前已经到达我们的转运中心，正在等待转运。

B: 转运中心？是什么意思？

H: 转运中心是一个中转站点，用于将包裹从发货地转运到目的地。在这个阶段，包裹可能需要等待一段时间，直到有足够的货物进行转运。

B: 那我什么时候能够知道包裹的最新状态呢？

H: 一般来说，我们会在包裹到达转运中心后更新其状态。你可以随时通过快递单号进行查询，或者等待我们给你发送最新的跟踪信息。

B: 好的。

H: 我们会尽快提供最新的跟踪信息。如果你有其他问题或需要帮助，请随时联系我们的客服部门。

Unit 4

投送包裹

Delivery of Parcel

投送包裹是指将包裹直接交付给收件人，在这个过程中需要与收件人进行有效的沟通和交流。有效的英语口语能够让交流更顺畅，并确保包裹安全交付。下面让我们一起来学习一下吧。

单词展示

fragile [ˈfrædʒaɪl] *adj.* 易碎的

courier [ˈkʊriə(r)] *n.* 送货员

insured [ɪnˈʃʊəd] *adj.* 投保的

service [ˈsɜːvɪs] *n.* 服务

address [əˈdres] *n.* 地址

notification [ˌnəʊtɪfɪˈkeɪʃn] *n.* 通知

street [striːt] *n.* 街道

details [ˈdiːteɪlz] *n.* 详情

change [tʃeɪndʒ] *n.* 变更

contact [ˈkɒntækt] *v.* 联系

句子示范

The package has been handed over to the courier company and is expected to be delivered to you within two days.

包裹已经交给快递公司，预计将在两天内送到您手中。

Please ensure that someone is available at home to receive the package for a successful delivery by the courier.

请确保有人在家接收包裹，以便快递员能够成功投递。

The delivery time of the package may be affected by weather or other uncontrollable factors, and we appreciate your understanding.

包裹的投送时间可能会受到天气或其他不可抗力因素的影响，请您谅解。

We will make every effort to ensure the safe delivery of your package. Thank you for your patience and wait.

我们会尽最大努力确保您的包裹安全投送，感谢您的耐心等待。

Celia 的包裹到了，快递员 Peter 通过电话联系 Celia，

与她确定包裹投递的具体事项。

C=Celia　　P=Peter

P: Hello, is that Celia?

C: Yes, this is Celia.

P: I'm a courier from Company A. I noticed that you have a package for delivery, and I'd like to confirm some delivery details.

C: Thank you for reaching out. What do you need to confirm?

P: Firstly, I need to confirm your exact delivery address to ensure accurate package delivery.

C: My delivery address is Unit ××, ×× Complex, 123 Street.

P: Alright. May I know the convenient delivery time for you?

C: I usually return home after 6 PM in the evening, so you can deliver the package during that time frame.

P: Okay, I will deliver the package to your address after 6 PM. If there are any changes or if I need to contact you in advance, I'll give you a call.

C: Thank you very much.

P: You're welcome. It's our responsibility. Have a pleasant day, goodbye.

P: 喂，请问是西莉亚吗？

C: 是的，我是西莉亚。

P: 我是 A 公司的快递员。我看到您有一个包裹需要投递，我想确认一些投递的事项。

C: 非常感谢您的来电。请问有什么需要确认的？

P: 首先，我需要确认您的具体收货地址，以便准确投递包裹。

C: 我的收货地址是 123 号街道，× × 小区，× × 单元。

P: 好的。请问您方便的投递时间是什么时候？

C: 我一般在晚上 6 点后回家，您可以在那个时间段投递。

P: 好的，晚上 6 点后我会将包裹送到您的地址。如果有什么变动或者需要提前联系您，我会打电话通知您的。

C: 非常感谢。

P: 不客气，这是我们的职责。祝您有一个愉快的一天，再见。

Unit 5

信息录入

Information Input

信息录入对于整个快递物流而言十分重要，所以掌握与之相关的英语表达很有必要。下面就来一起学习一下与信息录入相关的英语表达吧。

单词展示

input [ˈɪnpʊt] *n.* 输入

enter [ˈentə(r)] *v.* 输入

record [rɪˈkɔːd] *n.* 记录

database [ˈdeɪtəbeɪs] *n.* 数据库

save [seɪv] *v.* 保存

delete [dɪˈliːt] *v.* 删除

spreadsheet [ˈspredʃiːt] *n.* 电子表格

information [ˌɪnfəˈmeɪʃn] *n.* 信息

familiar [fəˈmɪliə(r)] *adj.* 熟悉的

omission [əˈmɪʃn] *n.* 省略

句子示范

We will validate the data you input to ensure its accuracy.

我们将会对您输入的数据进行验证，以确保其准确性。

After the courier information is entered, you will receive a text message containing the tracking number. You can use this number to track the progress of your package.

快递信息录入后，您将收到一条包含跟踪号码的短信，您可以使用该号码来查询包裹的进展。

When you sign for the package, we will request some necessary information for entry.

我们会在您签收包裹时要求您提供一些必要的信息，以便进行录入。

Once the courier information is entered, you can track the status of your package through the tracking system.

快递信息录入完成后，您可以通过查询系统来跟踪包裹的状态。

新员工 Dan 对录入信息还不太熟悉，便请教 Edwin 如

何录入。

D= Dan　　E=Edwin

D: Good morning, Edwin! I'm Dan, the new employee. I'm not familiar with entering information yet. Could you teach me?

E: No problem. First, we need to enter the input interface.

D: Understood.

E: In the input interface, we need to fill in the relevant information of the sender and receiver, including their names, contact details, addresses, and more. Make sure to input this information accurately and without errors.

D: I see. Any other important points to consider?

E: Another important step is entering delivery information. After completing a delivery, we need to record the time and personnel involved to facilitate tracking and statistics. The system has a specific function for entering delivery details. We need to input the delivery time, the delivery person, and associate it with the recipient's information.

D: Okay. Thank you for your guidance!

E: You're welcome! I'm glad to help you.

D: 早上好，爱德文！我是新来的丹，我还不太会录入信息，你能教我一下吗？

E: 没问题。首先，我们需要进入录入界面。

D: 明白。

E: 在录入界面，我们需要填写寄件人和收件人的相关信息，包括姓名、联系方式、地址等。确保准确无误地输入这些信息。

D: 明白了。还有其他需要注意的事项吗?

E: 还有一个重要的环节是录入送件信息。在完成送件后，我们需要记录送件的时间和人员信息，以便进行跟踪和统计。在系统中有相应的送件录入功能，我们需要输入送件的时间、派送人员等信息，并将其与收件人的信息进行关联。

D: 好的。非常感谢你的指导!

E: 不客气！很高兴能帮助你。

Chapter 4
绘画才艺

绘画是一种艺术形式，通过图像和色彩表达创作者的思想、情感和观点。随着各国之间文化交流的日益频繁，英语为绘画艺术的交流提供了重要的桥梁，无论是作品的解读、呈现还是评论，都需要准确而有力的英语表达。

Unit 1

选择绘画材料

Selecting Painting Material

在购买绘画材料时，绘画创作者可能需要询问关于材料的特性、用途、价格等方面的问题。流利的英语口语能够帮助他们准确理解和传达需求。

单词展示

easel [ˈiːzl] *n.* 画架，画布架

watercolors [ˈwɔːtə(r)ˌkʌlə(r)z] *n.* 水彩颜料

acrylics [əˈkrɪlɪks] *n.* 丙烯颜料

pencil [ˈpensl] *n.* 铅笔

ink [ɪŋk] *n.* 墨水

brush [brʌʃ] *n.* 刷子

gouache [guˈɑːʃ] *n.* 拉彩，粉彩

varnish [ˈvɑːrnɪʃ] *n.* 清漆

bristle [ˈbrɪsl] *n.* 刷毛

palette [ˈpælət] *n.* 调色板

句子示范

The bristles of this paintbrush are very soft, making it perfect for watercolor painting.

这支画笔的毛很柔软，非常适合水彩画。

I need a palette to mix the colors.

我需要一个调色板来混合颜色。

Considering portability, I have decided to purchase a folding easel.

考虑到便携性，我决定购买一个折叠式画架。

The texture and colors of oil paint are very rich.

油画颜料的质地和色彩非常丰富。

I am considering using charcoal pencil to enhance the light and dark effects of the artwork.

我正在考虑使用炭笔来增加画作的明暗效果。

Bonny 和 Elroy 需要完成绘画作业，假期他们来到艺术用品商店选购绘画材料。

B=Bonny   E=Elroy

B: Wow, there are so many art materials here! I'm looking to buy some new brushes and paints.

E: Yes, there's a wide selection here. What type of brushes and paints are you interested in?

B: I want to get a set of watercolor brushes and some watercolor paints.

E: Let's start by looking at the watercolor brushes. What type of brushes are you looking for? Soft bristle or stiff bristle?

B: I've heard that soft bristle brushes are suitable for watercolor painting as they allow better control of paint flow. Let's go find them.

E: Look, here are watercolor brushes in different sizes and shapes. You can try them out and see which one feels most comfortable for you.

B: Alright, I'll give them a try. This pointed brush looks nice. I think it can be used for detailing.

E: You'll also need some medium-sized and large-sized brushes for better application and color filling.

B: Right, I'll choose a few brushes that are suitable for different purposes.

E: Wow, there's such a wide variety of watercolor paints here. How many colors are you planning to get?

B: I want some basic colors like red, yellow, blue, and some neutral tones. That way, I can mix more colors.

B: 哇，这里的绘画材料真是琳琅满目啊！我正想买些新的画笔和颜料。

E: 是啊，这里的选择真的很多。你想买什么类型的画笔和颜料呢?

B: 我想买一套水彩画刷和一些水彩颜料。

E: 那我们先去看看水彩画刷吧。你想要什么类型的刷子？软毛的还是硬毛的?

B: 我听说软毛的刷子适合水彩画，可以更好地控制颜料的流动。我们去找一下。

E: 看，这里有不同尺寸和形状的水彩画刷。你可以试试看哪种手感最适合你。

B: 好的，我会试试看。这把尖头的刷子看起来不错，我觉得可以用来勾勒细节。

E: 那你还需要一些中等尺寸和大尺寸的刷子，以便更好地涂抹和填充颜色。

B: 没错，我会选几把适合不同用途的刷子。

E: 哇，这里的水彩颜料种类真是多得令人眼花缭乱。你打算选几种颜色?

B: 我想要一些基本颜色，比如红、黄、蓝以及一些中性色调。这样我可以混合出更多的颜色。

Unit 2

绘画创作

Painting Creation

通过流利的英语口语，能够与他人分享创作思想，与观众建立更深入的连接。下面让我们一起来学习一下吧。

单词展示

sketch [sketʃ] *n.* 素描；*v.* 草拟，画素描

shade [ʃeɪd] *n.* 阴影

perspective [pəˈspektɪv] *n.* 透视

contrast [ˈkɒntrɑːst] *n.* 对比，对照

highlight [ˈhaɪlaɪt] *n.* 突出部分，亮点

shadow [ˈʃædəʊ] *n.* 阴影；*v.* 投影，遮蔽

proportion [prəˈpɔːʃn] *n.* 比例

composition [ˌkɒmpəˈzɪʃn] *n.* 构图

asymmetric [ˌeɪsɪˈmetrɪk] *adj.* 不对称的

dynamism [ˈdaɪnəmɪzəm] *n.* 活力

句子示范

The use of colors in this painting is excellent, giving a bright and vivid feeling.

这幅画的色彩运用很出色，给人一种明亮而生动的感觉。

He employs bold color contrasts in his paintings, creating a strong visual impact.

他在绘画中运用了大胆的色彩对比，创造出了强烈的视觉效果。

This painting project requires us to express our views and concerns about social issues in a creative way.

这个绘画项目要求我们以创意的方式表达自己对社会问题的看法和关注。

He showcases a unique observation and understanding of the natural world through his paintings.

他通过绘画展现了对自然界的独特观察和理解。

Max 想要画一幅风景画，但不知道如何更好地构图，

便向老师 Crystal 请教。

M=Max C=Crystal

M: Teacher! I want to paint a landscape, but I don't know how to compose it better to express my ideas. Can I ask for your advice?

C: Of course. Composition is a crucial part of painting. First, you need to consider the overall balance and proportion of the composition. You can use some composition techniques to help you.

M: Okay.

C: First, consider the theme and focal point of the painting. What do you want the center of the painting to be? A tree? A mountain peak? Once you have determined the theme, you can emphasize it in the composition.

M: I want to highlight a mountain peak in the painting.

C: Then you can use symmetric or asymmetric composition. Symmetric composition can create a balanced and harmonious effect, while asymmetric composition can add dynamism and vitality to the painting.

M: I would like to try asymmetric composition to add some liveliness to the painting.

C: Additionally, pay attention to the lines and visual guidance in the painting. By utilizing the flow and direction of lines, you can guide the viewer's gaze and create a sense of depth in the painting.

M: How should I use lines to guide the viewer's gaze?

C: You can use the contour lines of the mountain peak or a pathway as elements to guide the viewer's gaze, allowing their eyes to naturally move from one part of the painting to another.

M: I understand.

C: Finally, consider the foreground, middle ground, and background of the painting to create a sense of depth. You can use size, contrast, and lighting to create a sense of perspective, immersing the viewer in the painting.

M: Thank you for your guidance! I have a better composition plan now, and I will strive to create an outstanding artwork.

M: 老师！我最近想画一幅风景画，但是我不知道如何构图才能更好地表达我的想法。能请教一下您吗？

C: 当然可以。构图是绘画中非常重要的一部分。首先，你需要考虑画面的整体平衡和比例。可以使用一些构图技巧来帮助你。

M: 好的。

C: 首先，考虑画面的主题和焦点。你希望画面的中心是什么？是一棵树？是一座山峰？确定好主题后，可以在构图中突出它。

M: 我想突出画面中的一座山峰。

C: 那么你可以使用对称或不对称的构图方式。对称构图可以使画面更加平衡，而不对称构图可以给画面增加一些动感和活力。

M: 我想尝试一下不对称构图，给画面增加一些活力。

C: 另外，要注意画面的线条和视觉引导。通过线条的走势和方向，可以引导观众的目光，使画面更加有层次感。

M: 那么我应该如何运用线条来引导视线呢？

C: 你可以利用山峰的轮廓线或者一条小径等线条元素来引导视线，让观众的目光自然地从画面的某个地方流动到另一个地方。

M: 明白了。

C: 最后，要考虑画面的前景、中景和背景，使它们形成层次感。可以利用大小、明暗对比等来创造景深效果，让观众有一种身临其境的感觉。

M: 谢谢您的指导！我现在有了更好的构图方案，我会努力创作出一幅出色的画作。

Unit 3

画作欣赏

Painting Appreciation

通过流利的英语口语，人们才能更好地理解和解读画作，对画作进行赏析。下面让我们一起来学习一下与画作欣赏相关的口语表达吧。

单词展示

artwork [ˈɑːtwɜːk] *n.* 艺术作品

aesthetics [iːsˈθɛtɪks] *n.* 美学

brushwork [ˈbrʌʃwɜːk] *n.* 画笔技法

detail [ˈdiːteɪl] *n.* 细节

harmony [ˈhɑːrməni] *n.* 和谐

depth [depθ] *n.* 深度

emotion [ɪˈməʊʃn] *n.* 情感

expression [ɪkˈspreʃn] *n.* 表现，表达

exhibition [ˌeksɪˈbɪʃn] *n.* 展览

interpretation [ɪnˌtɜːprəˈteɪʃn] *n.* 解释，解读

句子示范

Through delicate brushwork and layering, this painting expresses deep emotions and thoughts.

通过细腻的笔触和层次感，这幅画表达了深厚的情感和思想。

I am captivated by the color contrasts and shapes in this abstract painting, experiencing a strong visual impact.

我被这幅抽象画中的色彩对比和形状吸引，感受到了一种强烈的视觉冲击。

The attention to detail in this artwork is exquisite, with each detail showcasing the artist's dedication and skill.

这幅画中的细节处理非常精细，每个细节都展现了艺术家的用心和技巧。

I am moved by this artist's expressive approach, and every artwork is filled with unique emotions and ideas.

我被这位艺术家的表达方式打动，他的作品都充满了独特的情感和想法。

在绘画社团的活动中，三位成员聚在一起赏析毕加索的画作。

A=Ada　　B=Barbara　　E=Errol

A: Today, let's appreciate some of the great artist Picasso's artworks. I have prepared several of his representative pieces for you all.

E: Picasso's artistic style is unique and has influenced the development of modern art. Where should we begin our appreciation?

A: Let's start with "The Guitarist" . This painting is one of Picasso's works from his early Blue Period.

B: I notice the clean and flowing lines of the figures in the painting, and the blue tones evoke a sense of deep emotion. I feel that this artwork conveys a mood of solitude and introspection.

E: Yes, during Picasso's Blue Period, he expressed a lot of sadness and contemplation in his personal life. The composition of this painting is also interesting, with the posture of the guitarist echoing the background.

A: Next, let's look at "The Young Ladies of Avignon" . This painting is one of Picasso's representative works from his Cubist period.

B: Hmm, this painting has vibrant colors and a lively composition. I like the girl's smile and the natural elements behind her. It feels very cheerful.

E: This artwork showcases the characteristics of Cubism, where Picasso combines elements of both realism and abstract expressionism, creating rich visual effects.

A: The two artworks we just appreciated demonstrate Picasso's different artistic styles and creative approaches in various periods. By appreciating his paintings, we can gain a deeper understanding of the diversity and power of art.

A: 今天我们来一起赏析伟大艺术家毕加索的画作。我为大家准备了几幅他的代表作品。

E: 毕加索的艺术风格独特，引领了现代艺术的发展。我们从哪一幅作品开始赏析呢?

A: 让我们从《吉他手》开始吧。这幅画是毕加索早期蓝色时期的代表作之一。

B: 我注意到画中的人物线条简洁而流畅，而那种蓝色调给人一种深情的感觉。我觉得这幅作品传达了一种孤独与内省的情绪。

E: 对，蓝色时期的毕加索在他个人生活遭遇困境时表达了许多悲伤和思考。这幅画的构图也很有意思，吉他手的姿势和背景的关系相互呼应。

A: 接下来，我们来看《亚威农少女》。这幅画是毕加索的野兽派时期的代表之一。

B: 嗯，这幅画色彩鲜艳，画面充满活力。我喜欢画中女孩的微笑和她身后的自然元素，感觉非常欢快。

E: 这幅作品展现了野兽派的特点，毕加索将现实主义和抽象表现主义相结合，创造了丰富的视觉效果。

A: 我们刚才赏析的这两幅画作展示了毕加索不同阶段的艺术风格和创作思路。通过赏析他的画作，我们也能更深入地理解艺术的多样性和力量。

Unit 4

绘画比赛

Drawing Contests

英语能够帮助艺术家与比赛组织者进行有效的沟通。流利的英语口语能够帮助他们准确理解并遵守比赛规则，确保顺利参赛。下面让我们一起来学习一下吧。

单词展示

judging [ˈdʒʌdʒɪŋ] *n.* 评判

creativity [ˌkriːeɪˈtɪvəti] *n.* 创造力

contestant [kənˈtestənt] *n.* 参赛者

participate [pɑːˈtɪsɪpeɪt] *v.* 参与，参加

inspiration [ˌɪnspəˈreɪʃn] *n.* 灵感，启示

significance [sɪɡˈnɪfɪkəns] *n.* 重要性，意义

theme [θiːm] *n.* 主题

presentation [ˌpreznˈteɪʃn] *n.* 展示

honor [ˈɒnə(r)] *n.* 荣誉，尊敬

portrait [ˈpɔːtreɪt] *n.* 肖像，画像

句子示范

There are a large number of entries in this painting competition, making the competition very intense.

这次绘画比赛的参赛作品数量非常多，竞争非常激烈。

The judging panel will evaluate the entries based on creativity, technique, and expressiveness.

评审团将根据创意、技巧和表现力来评判参赛作品。

The composition and use of colors in this artwork showcase the artistic talent of the participant.

这幅作品的构图和色彩运用展现了参赛者的艺术才华。

The competition requires participants to utilize various techniques and materials to create their artworks.

比赛要求参赛者运用多种技巧和材料来创作作品。

The results of the competition will be announced at the award ceremony, and the winners will receive generous prizes.

比赛结果将在颁奖典礼上揭晓，获胜者将获得丰厚的奖品。

Bella 作为参赛者，参加了 A 杯绘画比赛，评委 Lily 就她的人物画给予了评价。

B=Bella L=Lily

B: Hello everyone, I'm Bella. It's an honor for me to participate in the A Cup Painting Competition. I have chosen portrait painting as my theme, aiming to express my emotions and ideas through my artwork.

L: Hello Bella. I just had the chance to admire your portrait painting, and I must say it left a deep impression on me. Could you share your inspiration and the significance behind your creation with us?

B: Certainly! The subject of this artwork is an elderly person whom I hold dear. I wanted to convey a sense of respect for wisdom, life experiences, and emotions through her image. Her expression, wrinkles, and gaze reflect the marks of time and the beauty of life.

L: You have successfully captured the emotions and life experiences of the subject. How did you approach the details and expressions of the portrait?

B: During the painting process, I used delicate lines and gradients of color to depict the facial features and expressions of the subject. I focused on capturing the wisdom and determination in her gaze, and used colors to express her inner emotions.

L: Your execution is exceptional, with meticulous attention to detail. Your painting evokes a sense of contemplation and introspection. Did you encounter any challenges during the painting process?

B: I did face some challenges during the creative process. Especially in capturing the expressions and subtle changes in the subject, it required a lot of time and effort in studying and practicing. However, these challenges have helped me grow and improve.

L: It's a wonderful growth process. Your artwork conveys profound emotions and meaning. I believe your creativity will continue to flourish. Thank you for sharing.

B: Thank you very much for your evaluation and encouragement. I believe that painting is a powerful form of expression. I will continue to strive in my artistic journey and share more stories and emotions with the audience.

B: 大家好，我是贝拉，很荣幸参加 A 杯绘画比赛。我选择了人物画作为我的创作主题，希望能通过绘画表达出自己的情感和理念。

L: 你好，贝拉。我刚刚欣赏了你的人物画，我必须说它给我留下了深刻的印象。你能跟我们分享一下你的创作灵感和意义吗？

B: 当然！这幅画作中的人物是我亲近的一位长者。我希望通过她的形象传达出对智慧、经历和情感的尊重。她的表情、皱纹和眼神中透露出岁月的痕迹和生活的韵味。

L: 你成功地捕捉到了人物的情感和生活经历。你是如何处理人物的细节和表情的?

B: 在绘画过程中，我用了细腻的线条和渐变的色彩来刻画人物的面部特征和表情。我注重捕捉她眼神中的智慧和坚毅，并通过色彩的运用来表达她的内心情感。

L: 你的处理非常出色，细节表现得非常精细。这幅画给人一种沉思和思考的感觉。你在绘画过程中有没有遇到什么挑战?

B: 在创作过程中，我确实遇到了一些挑战。尤其是要捕捉到人物的表情和细微的变化，需要我花费很多时间和精力来研究和实践。但是，这种挑战也让我不断进步和提高。

L: 这是很好的成长过程。你的作品传达出了深沉的情感和内涵。我相信你的创作会继续有更大的发展。谢谢你的分享。

B: 非常感谢您的评价和鼓励。我相信绘画是一种强大的表达方式，我会继续努力创作，并通过我的画作与观众分享更多故事和情感。

Unit 5

参观画展

A Visit to Art Exhibition

具备良好的英语口语能力，可以在参观画展的过程中更好地就画作进行交流，更好地解读和欣赏画展作品，下面就一起来学习相关的表达吧。

单词展示

gallery [ˈɡæləri] *n.* 画廊

curator [kjʊəˈreɪtə(r)] *n.* 馆长，策展人

masterpiece [ˈmɑːstəpiːs] *n.* 杰作

critique [krɪˈtiːk] *n.* 评论

visitor [ˈvɪzɪtə(r)] *n.* 访客

appreciation [əˌpriːʃiˈeɪʃn] *n.* 欣赏

breathtaking [ˈbreθteɪkɪŋ] *adj.* 惊人的

dreamlike [ˈdriːmlaɪk] *adj.* 如梦似幻的

fascinated [ˈfæsɪneɪtɪd] *adj.* 入迷的

charm [tʃɑːm] *n.* 魅力

句子示范

When visiting the art exhibitions, we can appreciate artworks of various styles and themes.

参观画展时，我们可以欣赏到各种不同风格和主题的艺术作品。

I particularly admire that oil painting, where the artist expresses intense emotions through colors and details.

我特别喜欢那幅油画，画家通过色彩和细节表达了强烈的情感。

Visiting art exhibitions not only allows us to appreciate artworks but also helps us understand the artists' creative concepts and the stories behind their works.

参观画展不仅可以欣赏艺术作品，还能了解艺术家的创作理念和背后的故事。

Daisy 和 Fiona 相约一起去美术馆看最近的画展，她们对那些知名画作进行了赏析。

D=Daisy　　F=Fiona

D: Let’s go to an art exhibition today! I heard there are some famous painters’ works on display.

F: That’s great! I heard there are several paintings by Vincent van Gogh in the exhibition. I’m really looking forward to seeing his unique colors and expressiveness.

D: Wow, this “Starry Night” is truly breathtaking! Van Gogh creates a dreamlike night sky scene with swirling brushstrokes and vibrant colors.

F: Yes, his heavy brushstrokes seem to convey the passion and anguish from deep within him. The stars and the moon in the painting shimmer with a mysterious glow.

D: Come and see, this is Monet’s “Water Lilies” . It gives a tranquil and serene feeling. The artist creates an enchanting water landscape with the gradients of color and the reflection on the water’s surface.

F: Absolutely! He employs bold color contrasts to showcase the beauty and harmony of the natural world. I can almost smell the fragrance of those water lilies.

D: This exhibition has made me even more fascinated by art. Each artwork has brought me different feelings and thoughts.

F: Yes, the charm of art lies in its ability to touch our innermost emotions and thoughts. I hope we’ll have more opportunities to appreciate artworks in the future.

D: 今天我们一起去看画展吧！听说有一些知名画家的作品在展出。

F: 太好了！我听说展览中有几幅凡·高的画作，我很期待看到他那独特的色彩和表现力。

D: 哇，这幅《星夜》真是令人惊叹！凡·高通过旋转的笔触和明亮的色彩，创造出了一个梦幻般的星空景象。

F: 是的，他用那种厚重的笔触，仿佛能感受到他内心深处的热情和痛苦。画面中的星星和月亮都闪烁着神秘的光芒。

D: 快来看，这是莫奈的《睡莲》，这幅画真是给人一种平静而宁谧的感觉。画家通过色彩的渐变和水面的倒影，营造出了一个宛如仙境般的水景。

F: 没错！他在画作中运用了大胆的色彩对比，展现出了自然界的美丽与和谐。我仿佛能闻到那片睡莲花的清香。

D: 这次画展真是让我对艺术更加着迷了。每幅作品都带给我不同的感受和思考。

F: 是啊，艺术的魅力就在于它能触动我们内心深处的情感和思想。我希望以后还能有机会欣赏更多的艺术作品。

Chapter 5 音乐艺术

音乐是一种跨文化的艺术形式，而英语作为国际通用语言在音乐领域扮演着重要的角色。在音乐制作、演唱或创作过程中，英语都被广泛应用。掌握良好的英语口语能力能够促进音乐团队之间的顺畅沟通和协作，提高音乐作品的质量和影响力。

Unit 1

歌唱练习

Singing Practice

歌唱练习有助于培养良好的呼吸技巧和音域，增强音乐感知和演唱技巧。恰当的英语口语表达可以帮助我们更好地交流歌唱练习的技巧，下面就一起来学习一下吧。

单词展示

vocalization [ˌvəʊkəlaɪˈzeɪʃn] *n.* 发声	volume [ˈvɒljuːm] *n.* 音量，响度
breath [breθ] *n.* 呼吸，气息	harmony [ˈhɑːməni] *n.* 和谐，协调
range [reɪndʒ] *n.* 音域	projection [prəˈdʒekʃn] *n.* 发声力度
articulation [ɑːˌtɪkjuˈleɪʃn] *n.* 发音清晰度	resonance [ˈrezənəns] *n.* 共鸣，共振
pitch [pɪtʃ] *n.* 音高，音调	rhythm [ˈrɪðəm] *n.* 节奏

句子示范

When practicing singing, it is important to pay attention to breath control and vocal techniques.

歌唱练习时要注意呼吸控制和发声技巧。

During singing practice, emphasis should be placed on pitch accuracy and a sense of rhythm.

练习歌唱时要注重音准和节奏感。

Beginners can improve pronunciation and clarity by practicing repeatedly.

初学者可以通过反复练习来改善发音和咬字清晰度。

When practicing vocal segments, it is important to focus on correct tone and volume control.

练习唱段时要注意正确的音色和音量控制。

Prior to participating in a singing competition, systematic practice and stage performance training are necessary.

参加歌唱比赛前要进行系统的练习和舞台表演训练。

在排练室里，Alistair 正耐心地指导着新人歌手 Georgina 的歌唱练习。

A=Alistair G=Georgina

A: Georgina, today we're going to discuss some important singing techniques and considerations. First, let's talk about breath control. Do you know how crucial it is in singing?

G: Yes, I've heard about it, but I'm not quite sure how to do it.

A: Let me demonstrate. First, relax your body, stand up straight, and take a deep breath, feeling your abdomen expand without excessive tension in your chest. Then, exhale slowly, trying to prolong the exhale. This can help you maintain a steady airflow, making your singing more stable and powerful.

G: Got it. I'll give it a try.

A: Great. Next, let's discuss pitch accuracy and sense of rhythm. In singing, precise pitch and steady rhythm are vital.

G: I think I have a lot of room for improvement in that aspect.

A: That's okay. It can be improved through practice. You can use a piano or other instruments to help train your sense of pitch. Additionally, listen to talented singers as much as possible to learn from their sense of rhythm and expression.

G: Okay, I'll try to listen and learn more. Are there any other aspects I should pay attention to?

A: Pay attention to vocal resonance, which means allowing the sound to resonate in different parts of your body, creating a fuller sound.

G: I understand. Thank you for your guidance.

A: You're welcome, Georgina. Learning to sing takes patience and perseverance. As long as you keep practicing and actively absorb experiences, you will definitely make progress.

A: 乔治娜，我们今天来讨论一些重要的唱歌技巧和注意事项。首先，我们要谈谈呼吸控制。你知道在歌唱中，正确的呼吸有多么重要吗?

G: 是的，我听说过，但我还不太确定怎么做。

A: 我来给你示范一下。首先，放松你的身体，站直，然后深吸一口气，感觉腹部膨胀，胸部不要过分用力。接着，缓慢地呼气，尽量延长呼气时间。这样做可以帮助你保持稳定的气流，使你的歌声更加稳定而富有力量。

G: 明白了，我试试看。

A: 很好。接下来，我们要谈谈音准和节奏感。在歌唱中，准确的音准和稳定的节奏是非常重要的。

G: 我想我在这方面还有很大的提升空间。

A: 没关系，这是可以通过练习来改善的。你可以使用钢琴或其他乐器来帮助你锻炼音准感。同时，尽量多听一些优秀歌手的演唱，学习他们的节奏感和表达方式。

G: 好的，我会尽量多听多学。还有其他方面我需要注意的吗？

A: 要注重声音的共鸣，即让声音在身体的不同部位共鸣出来，使歌声更加丰满。

G: 我明白了。谢谢您的指导。

A: 不客气，乔治娜。学习歌唱需要耐心和坚持，只要你保持练习并积极吸收经验，你一定会进步的。

Unit 2

纠正发音

Pronunciation Correction

准确的发音对于歌曲的表达和理解至关重要，那么与之相关的英语表达你知道多少呢？下面就一起来学习一下吧。

单词展示

pronunciation [prəˌnʌnsiˈeɪʃn] *n.* 发音	tongue [tʌŋ] *n.* 舌头
diction [ˈdɪkʃn] *n.* 措辞，发音准确性	vowel [ˈvaʊəl] *n.* 元音
consonant [ˈkɒnsənənt] *n.* 辅音	nasality [neɪˈzælɪti] *n.* 鼻音，鼻腔共鸣
clarity [ˈklærəti] *n.* 清晰度，清楚度	accent [ˈæksent] *n.* 口音，腔调
lyric [ˈlɪrɪk] *n.* 歌词	accurate [ˈækjərət] *adj.* 准确的，精确的

句子示范

It is important to pay attention to correcting pronunciation while singing to ensure clarity and accuracy.

歌唱时要注意纠正发音，确保清晰准确。

Inaccurate pronunciation can affect the expression and communication of the song.

发音不准确会影响歌曲的表达力和沟通效果。

Pay attention to tongue position and mouth shape, especially when singing English songs.

要注意舌位和口型，特别是唱英文歌时。

You can use pronunciation exercise software or recording devices to self-correct while practicing pronunciation.

练习发音时可以使用语音练习软件或录音设备来自我纠正。

Sometimes, it is necessary to practice specific syllables or words repeatedly to improve pronunciation.

有时候需要反复练习某个音节或单词来改善发音。

在音乐教室里，音乐老师 Felicity 正在给学生们上课。今天的课程内容是关于发音的重要性。

F=Felicity　　G=Ginny　　A=Allen

F: Students, today we're going to talk about the importance of pronunciation in singing. Accurate and clear pronunciation is crucial for effective vocal expression. Whether it's a Chinese song or a foreign language song, it's important to pay attention to accurate pronunciation, so that the audience can understand the lyrics. Please listen carefully.

G: Teacher, I always have trouble with accurate pronunciation when practicing singing. Are there any methods to improve?

F: That's a great question! To correct pronunciation issues, first, you need to pay attention to tongue placement and mouth shape. Especially for foreign language songs, observe the vowels and consonants in the lyrics and practice the correct pronunciation. You can listen to recordings, imitate the pronunciation of excellent singers, and use pronunciation practice apps to help you correct it.

A: Teacher, sometimes my pronunciation becomes unclear when singing high notes. What should I do?

F: Unclear pronunciation when singing high notes may be due to excessive tension in the throat or insufficient resonance. You can try to relax your throat and pay attention to the correct vocal techniques. Additionally, focus on vocal resonance, allowing the sound to resonate in different parts of your body, creating a fuller and more powerful singing voice.

(*Felicity walks to each student in the class and points out their pronunciation issues.*)

F: Ginny, you need to make your pronunciation clearer when singing, and pay attention to tongue placement control. Smoothly transition between syllables and avoid any regional accents. Allen, your vowel pronunciation is a bit unclear, try elongating the syllables to improve it. Your "R" pronunciation can be clearer as well.

F: 同学们，今天我们要谈谈唱歌中发音的重要性。一个准确清晰的发音对于歌唱表达是至关重要的。无论是中文歌曲还是外语歌曲，都需要注意准确发音，以便让观众能够听懂你们的歌词。请大家注意听好。

G: 老师，我平时练习唱歌时发音总是不太准确，有什么方法可以改善吗？

F: 很好的问题！要纠正发音问题，首先需要注意舌位和口型。

特别是对于外语歌曲，要注意观察歌词中的元音和辅音，并练习正确的发音方式。可以多听录音，模仿优秀歌手的发音，还可以使用一些发音练习 App 来帮助你纠正。

A: 老师，我有时候唱高音时会发音模糊，怎么办？

F: 唱高音时发音模糊可能是由于喉咙过度用力或共鸣不足导致的。你可以试着放松喉咙，注意正确的发声技巧。同时，要注重声音的共鸣，让声音在身体的不同部位共鸣出来，使你的歌声更加丰满而富有力量。

（费莉希蒂走到班上的每位学生旁边，指出他们的发音问题。）

F: 金妮，你唱歌时发音需要更清晰一些，注意舌位的控制。注意平滑过渡音节，避免带有方言口音。艾伦，你的元音发音有些模糊，尝试拉长音节来改善。你的字母“R”发音可以再清晰一些。

Unit 3

文艺表演

Art Performance

文艺表演是一种以艺术形式呈现的表演活动，包括多种形式。下面就来学习一下与文艺表演相关的英语表达吧。

单词展示

performance [pəˈfɔːməns] *n.* 表演，演出

artistry [ˈɑːtɪstri] *n.* 艺术才华，艺术性

stage [steɪdʒ] *n.* 舞台

acting [ˈæktɪŋ] *n.* 演技，表演

dance [dɑːns] *n.* 舞蹈

music [ˈmjuːzɪk] *n.* 音乐

venue [ˈvenjuː] *n.* 场地，演出地点

tuning [ˈtjuːnɪŋ] *n.* 调音

costume [ˈkɒstjuːm] *n.* 服装

repair [rɪˈpeə(r)] *v.* 修复

句子示范

In artistic performances, actors demonstrate exceptional performance skills and heartfelt emotions.

在文艺表演中，演员们展现出了卓越的表演技巧和感人的情感。

Tonight's concert is a splendid artistic performance. Let's enjoy it together!

今晚的音乐会是一场精彩的文艺表演，我们一起来欣赏吧！

Every participation in artistic performances is a challenge and opportunity for me to enhance my performance abilities.

每次参加文艺表演都是对我表演能力的一次挑战和提升。

During the performance, artists transport the audience to a whole new artistic world through their exquisite skills and expressive power.

演出时艺术家们通过精湛的技艺和表达力，将观众带入了一个全新的艺术世界。

We need to improve the actors' performance level and overall stage effect through continuous rehearsals.

我们需要通过不断的排练来提高演员们的表演水平和整体舞台效果。

在一场即将开始的音乐文艺表演的后台，舞台经理 Jessica 与音乐指导 Bryan、服装设计师 Arthur 以及灯光师 Kate 一起商量组织这场表演的注意事项。

J=Jessica B=Bryan A=Arthur K=Kate

J: Hello, everyone! Thank you very much for attending this organizational meeting for the music and arts performance. We want to ensure a smooth execution of this show. Are there any specific matters we need to pay special attention to?

B: First, in terms of music, we need to ensure accurate tuning of the instruments, harmonious performance of the music pieces, and coordination with the singers and dance team to ensure harmony between the music and the dance.

A: Regarding costume design, I have prepared costumes for each performer, but we need everyone's assistance in checking if the sizes are appropriate, if any damaged parts need repair, and if they match the performance scenes.

K: In terms of lighting, we need to adjust the brightness, colors, and effects of the lights according to different scenes and performance content to highlight the focal points and create the desired atmosphere. Additionally, we should pay attention to the safe use of lighting equipment, avoiding fire hazards and visual discomfort for the audience.

J: Excellent, we have covered music, costumes, and lighting. Are there any other aspects we need to consider?

B: I think we need to ensure sufficient rehearsal time for the performers. They need to become familiar with the stage and the use of stage props, while also coordinating with the orchestra, choir, and other artists.

A: Yes, we also need to ensure that the performers' movements on stage are smooth and natural, and their costumes are appropriate for their roles and the performance requirements.

K: I would also like to remind everyone about the safety of the stage props. We need to ensure that the props are stable and comply with fire safety requirements, avoiding any unforeseen incidents.

A: That's an important reminder! We also need to prepare the sound equipment to ensure clear audio transmission to the audience without any noise or poor sound quality.

B: Lastly, we must remember to take care of the audience reception, ensuring that they can enjoy a splendid arts performance and have a great viewing experience.

J: Thank you all for your suggestions and reminders! We will work closely together to ensure the success and excellence of this music and arts performance.

J: 大家好！非常感谢你们能来参加这次音乐文艺表演的组织会议。我们要确保这场表演的顺利进行，有没有什么需要特别注意的事项？

B: 首先，音乐方面，我们要确保乐器的调音准确，乐曲的演奏和合唱的和谐。还有，要与歌手和舞蹈团队密切配合，确保音乐和舞蹈的协调性。

A: 对于服装设计，我已经准备好了每个演员的服装，但需要大家协助检查尺寸是否合适，是否有损坏的部分需要修复，以及是否与演出场景相符。

K: 在灯光方面，我们要根据不同场景和表演内容调整灯光的亮度、色彩和效果，以突出表演的重点和氛围。另外，注意安全使用灯光设备，避免火灾和观众的视觉不适。

J: 非常好，我们已经覆盖了音乐、服装和灯光。还有其他方面需要考虑吗？

B: 我觉得我们需要确保演员们的排练时间充足，他们需要熟悉舞台和舞台布景的运用，同时还要与乐队、合唱团和其他艺术家们进行协调。

A: 对，我们还要确保演员们在舞台上的舞步和动作流畅自然，服装的穿着也要符合角色和表演的要求。

K: 我还想提醒大家关于舞台布景的安全，要确保布景稳固并符合防火要求，避免发生任何意外情况。

A: 非常重要的提醒！我们还要准备好音响设备，确保声音能清晰传达给观众，不要有任何杂音或不良音质。

B: 最后，我们要记得做好观众的接待工作，确保他们能够享受到一场精彩的文艺表演，获得良好的观赏体验。

J: 非常感谢大家的建议和提醒！我们会密切合作，确保这场音乐文艺表演的成功和精彩。

Unit 4

欣赏音乐会

Enjoying the Concert

欣赏音乐是一件陶冶情操、十分惬意的事情，与之相关的英语表达十分丰富，下面就一起来学习一下吧。

单词展示

auditorium [ˌɔːdɪˈtɔːriəm] *n.* 礼堂，观众席

symphony [ˈsɪmfəni] *n.* 交响乐，交响曲

soloist [ˈsəʊləʊɪst] *n.* 独奏者，独唱者

conductor [kənˈdʌktə(r)] *n.* 指挥家

applause [əˈplɔːz] *n.* 鼓掌，喝彩

tempo [ˈtempəʊ] *n.* 速度，拍子

rehearsal [rɪˈhɜːsl] *n.* 排练，彩排

concert [ˈkɒnsət] *n.* 音乐会

impeccable [ɪmˈpekəbl] *adj.* 无可挑剔的

coordination [kəʊˌɔːrdɪˈneɪʃn] *n.* 协调

句子示范

The performance skills in this concert are remarkably exquisite, and each instrument produces a delightful sound.

这场音乐会的演奏技巧非常精湛，每个乐器都发出了悦耳的声音。

The musicians interpret the music with their heart and skills, creating a captivating experience that is truly enchanting.

演奏家们用心灵和技巧将音乐演绎得如此精彩，令人陶醉其中。

The audience applauds and pays tribute during the concert, expressing their appreciation and admiration for the musicians.

观众们在音乐会上鼓掌致敬，表达对音乐家们的赞赏和喜爱。

I always look forward to the arrival of concerts because it provides an opportunity to be in close proximity to the musicians.

我常常期待着音乐会的到来，因为那是一次与音乐家们近距离接触的机会。

Every time I attend a concert, I am deeply moved by the musicians' skill and emotions.

每次去音乐会，我都会被演奏家们的技艺和情感所打动。

晚上，Jennifer 和 Lucia 相约一起去听音乐会。听完音乐会后，她们一起交流心得。

J=Jennifer　　L=Lucia

J: Tonight's concert was absolutely amazing! I never imagined that music could be so moving, and my understanding of classical music has deepened.

L: Yes, this was my first time attending a symphony orchestra performance, and it was truly awe-inspiring. The conductor's conducting skills were incredible, and the performance of each instrument was exquisite.

J: My favorite was Beethoven's "Symphony No. 9" . The coordination between the choir and the orchestra was impeccable, especially in the final choral section, which brought tears to my eyes.

L: I loved it too! During the final chorus, I felt like I was immersed in a solemn and profound scene, experiencing the power of music. That exhilarating feeling was amazing!

J: And the violinist, her skill was extraordinary. When she performed

“Butterfly Lovers”, I couldn’t help but be drawn into her musical world, feeling as if I were part of that moving love story.

L: Absolutely, her performance was breathtaking. Every note from her violin was so melodious and captivating, and it made me appreciate the beauty and depth of love.

J: Besides the music itself, the overall atmosphere of the concert was fantastic. Everyone was fully engaged in the music, applauding warmly from time to time, creating a rich artistic ambiance.

L: I completely agree. The power of music is irresistible. It touches the depths of our emotions and makes us love life even more.

J: 今晚的音乐会真是太精彩了！我从未想过音乐能够如此感人，我对古典音乐的认识也更深了。

L: 是的，我也是第一次来听交响乐演奏，这次体验真是太震撼了。指挥家的指挥技巧真是非常了不起，每个乐器的演奏都如此精湛。

J: 我最喜欢的是那首贝多芬的《第九交响曲》。合唱团和交响乐团的配合非常默契，尤其是最后的合唱部分，让我感动得热泪盈眶。

L: 我也很喜欢那首！在最后的合唱中，我仿佛置身于一个庄严肃穆的场景，感受到了音乐的力量。那种振奋人心的感觉真是太棒了！

J: 还有那位小提琴演奏家，她的琴艺真是太高超了。在演奏

《梁祝》的时候，我不禁陷入了她音乐的世界，感觉自己仿佛也在那动人的爱情故事里。

L: 没错，她的演奏技巧真是让人叹为观止。每一声琴音都如此悠扬动听，她的演奏让我感受到了爱情的美好和深沉。

J: 除了乐曲本身，整个音乐会的氛围也非常棒。大家都投入音乐中，不时发出热烈的掌声，营造出了一种浓厚的艺术氛围。

L: 我完全同意。音乐的魔力真是令人难以抗拒，它能够触动我们内心深处的情感，让我们更加热爱生活。

Chapter 6 体育运动

体育运动是培养身体素质的各种活动。如果掌握流利的英语口语，就可以在体育运动中轻松地与他人交流、合作，更好地开展体育运动。所以，掌握与体育运动相关的英语表达是非常有必要的。

Unit 1

热身活动

Warming-up

热身活动是在开展体育运动前进行的一系列准备性活动，旨在预防运动伤害和提高身体机能。下面就来学习一些与热身活动相关的英语表达吧。

单词展示

warm-up [ˈwɔːvm ʌp] *n./v.* 热身

stretch [stretʃ] *n./v.* 拉伸

exercise [ˈeksəsaɪz] *n./v.* 锻炼

mobility [məʊˈbɪləti] *n.* 移动性，灵活性

agility [əˈdʒɪlɪti] *n.* 敏捷，灵活性

strength [streŋθ] *n.* 力量，强度

coordination [kəʊˌɔːdɪˈneɪʃn] *n.* 协调，配合

breathing [ˈbriːðɪŋ] *n.* 呼吸

cardiovascular [ˌkɑːdiəʊˈvæskjələ(r)] *adj.* 心血管的

flexibility [ˌfleksəˈbɪləti] *n.* 灵活性，柔韧性

句子示范

Warming-up before engaging in any sports activity is crucial as it helps prevent injuries.

在进行任何体育活动之前，做热身活动都是很重要的，它可以预防受伤。

Warm-up exercises include stretching, jumping, and rotating movements, which enhance flexibility and blood circulation in the body.

热身活动包括伸展、跳跃和旋转等动作，可以提高身体的灵活性，促进血液循环。

During the warm-up process, we can perform simple exercises such as running, squats, and push-ups.

在热身过程中，我们可以做跑步、深蹲和俯卧撑等简单的运动。

Warm-up activities help increase muscle temperature and elasticity, making our muscles and joints more mobile.

热身活动有助于增加肌肉的温度和弹性，使我们的肌肉和关节更灵活。

By warming-up, we can prevent muscle strains, sprains, and other sports-related injuries.

通过热身活动，我们可以预防肌肉拉伤、扭伤和其他运动损伤。

在体育课上，Andy 老师准备教学生们做热身活动。

A=Andy M=Maisie B=Bonny

A: Hello, everyone! Before starting the exercise, let's start with a warm-up activity. First of all, warm-up exercises are very important for our bodies as they help prevent sports injuries and improve exercise effectiveness. Do you know the benefits of warm-up activities?

M: Teacher, warm-up activities can increase muscle temperature and flexibility, preventing injuries.

A: Excellent! Does anyone else have any understanding of warm-up activities?

B: Warm-up activities can also increase heart rate and breathing frequency, preparing the body for exercise.

A: Absolutely right! Now, let's start the warm-up activities together! We will begin with some simple jogging exercises to accelerate heart rate and blood circulation. Now, everyone jog slowly while maintaining even breathing.

(*Students jog while breathing, gradually getting their bodies accustomed to exercise.*)

A: Very good! Next, let's do some stretching exercises to increase muscle flexibility. Raise both arms and extend your right arm across your body towards the left side. Hold your left hand at your right elbow and feel the stretch in your shoulders. Repeat the same process on the opposite side. Fantastic! Now, let's do some squats to engage the thigh and gluteal muscles. Maintain balance during squats, ensuring that your knees do not go beyond your toes. How do you feel?

M: I feel warm in my body and ready to start exercising.

B: I feel more flexible, and I don't feel as tense during exercise.

A: 同学们，大家好！在开始运动之前，我们先来进行热身活动。热身活动对我们的身体非常重要，可以帮助我们预防运动伤害，提高运动效果。你们知道热身活动的作用吗？

M: 老师，热身活动可以增加肌肉的温度和灵活性，预防受伤。

A: 非常好！还有其他同学对热身活动有什么了解吗？

B: 热身活动还可以提高心率和呼吸频率，让身体做好准备。

A: 非常正确！现在，我们一起开始热身活动吧！我们先来做一些简单的跑步活动，这样可以加快心率和血液循环。现在，大家一起慢跑，记得保持均匀的呼吸。

（学生们一边慢跑一边呼吸，身体逐渐适应运动状态。）

A: 很好！接下来，我们来做一些伸展活动，可以增加肌肉的灵活性。大家举起双臂，右臂越过身体伸向左侧，左手固定于右手肘处，感受肩部的拉伸，对侧方法相同。非常棒！现在，我们来做一些下蹲活动，可以活动大腿和臀部肌肉。大家下蹲时保持身体平衡，注意膝盖不要超过脚尖。你们感觉如何？

M: 感觉身体暖和了，准备好开始运动了。

B: 我觉得身体变得灵活了，运动时不那么紧绷了。

Unit 2

运动锻炼

Exercise

掌握与运动锻炼相关的英语表达，可以使自己在运动中沟通更顺畅，表现更出色。下面就来学习一些关于运动锻炼的英语表达吧。

单词展示

stamina [ˈstæmɪnə] *n.* 耐力，持久力

training [ˈtreɪnɪŋ] *n.* 训练，培训

gym [dʒɪm] *n.* 健身房

sports [spɔːts] *n.* 运动，体育

muscles [ˈmʌslz] *n.* 肌肉

resistance [rɪˈzɪstəns] *n.* 抵抗，阻力

repetitions [ˌrɛpɪˈtɪʃənz] *n.* 重复

endurance [ɪnˈdjʊərəns] *n.* 耐力

suggestion [səˈdʒestʃən] *n.* 建议，提议

weight [weɪt] *n.* 重量，体重

句子示范

Consistently exercising every day can improve overall fitness levels.

坚持每天锻炼可以提高身体的健康水平。

Physical exercise can enhance muscle strength and endurance.

运动锻炼可以增强肌肉力量和耐力。

Aerobic exercise can improve cardiovascular health and promote blood circulation.

有氧运动可以改善心肺功能，促进血液循环。

During physical education classes, we typically engage in various physical training exercises to enhance our physical fitness.

体育课上，我们通常会进行各种体能训练来增强体质。

Gyms offer a variety of equipment that can assist us in achieving comprehensive body workouts.

健身房里有各种器械，可以帮助我们进行全面的身体锻炼。

在健身房里，Bob 正在专注地进行举重训练。健身教练

Colin 走过来，向他打招呼。

B=Bob　　C=Colin

C: Hi there! I noticed you're exercising. Do you need any help?

B: Hi, thanks! Actually, I'm trying to increase my muscle strength, but I feel like progress is slow. Do you have any suggestions?

C: Of course! First, you need to make sure your training plan sufficiently challenges your muscles. Try increasing weight or changing exercise methods appropriately to stimulate muscle growth.

B: Alright, I'll try increasing the weight. Are there any other exercises that can help me increase muscle strength?

C: In addition to weight training, you can also try compound exercises. These movements activate multiple muscle groups simultaneously, helping you develop overall strength.

B: Understood! Any recommendations regarding rest?

C: Certainly! Adequate rest is also essential when increasing muscle strength. Give yourself enough time to recover, allowing muscles to repair and grow.

B: Thank you very much for your advice!

C: You're welcome!

C: 嗨，你好！我看你在这里锻炼，需要一些帮助吗？

B: 嗨，谢谢！其实我正在尝试增加我的肌肉力量，但感觉进展缓慢。你有什么建议吗？

C: 当然！首先，你要确保你的训练计划充分挑战你的肌肉。尝试适当增加重量或改变练习方式，以激发肌肉的增长。

B: 好的，我会尝试增加重量。还有其他的锻炼方法可以帮助我增加肌肉力量吗？

C: 除了重量训练，你也可以尝试一些复合动作。这些动作可以同时激活多个肌肉群，帮助你全面发展力量。

B: 明白了！还有关于休息的建议吗？

C: 当然！在增加肌肉力量时，适当的休息也非常重要。给自己足够的时间恢复，让肌肉有时间修复和增长。

B: 非常感谢你的建议！

C: 不客气！

Unit 3

参加比赛

Entering the Competition

在参加比赛时，需要与裁判、队友和对手进行交流，包括了解比赛规则、进行战术安排以及比赛中的沟通和协作。这就需要掌握与比赛相关的英语表达。下面就一起来学习一下吧。

单词 展示

contest [ˈkɒntest, kənˈtest] *n./v.* 竞赛，比赛

tournament [ˈtʊənəmənt] *n.* 锦标赛，比赛

race [reɪs] *n./v.* 竞赛，比赛

match [mætʃ] *n./v.* 比赛，对阵

game [ɡeɪm] *n./v.* 游戏，比赛

athlete [ˈæθliːt] *n.* 运动员

team [tiːm] *n.* 球队，团队

victory [ˈvɪktəri] *n.* 胜利，成功

championship [ˈtʃæmpiənʃɪp] *n.* 冠军赛，锦标赛

defeat [dɪˈfiːt] *n./v.* 失败，战胜

句子示范

As the captain, I will lead our basketball team to participate in the regional championship.

作为队长，我会带领我们的篮球队参加区域锦标赛。

We will train hard and strive to achieve good results in the competition.

我们要尽全力训练，争取在比赛中取得好成绩。

Participating in the competition is not only an opportunity to showcase ourselves but also a chance to learn and exchange with other players.

参加比赛不仅是展示自己的机会，也是与其他选手交流学习的机会。

During the competition, we will demonstrate the spirit of teamwork, supporting and cooperating with each other.

在比赛中，我们要展现出团队合作的精神，互相支持和配合。

在体育馆内，教练 Ernest 正在和队员们进行比赛前的训

练和准备。队员们集中注意力聆听教练的指导。

E=Ernest A=Aaron B=Bertram C=Cyril

E: Hello, everyone! Tomorrow, we will be participating in an important basketball game, and I'd like to share some important points and professional requirements with all of you.

A: Coach, please tell us about the things we need to pay attention to and the skills required during the game.

E: First and foremost, it is crucial to warm up adequately before the game to ensure that your body is in optimal condition. This helps prevent injuries and improves body's flexibility and responsiveness.

B: Coach, are there any specific skills we need to master during the game?

E: In the game, teamwork is extremely important. You should constantly communicate and cooperate with your teammates, ensuring good coordination in passing and defense. Additionally, accurate shooting and quick responsiveness are crucial for winning.

C: Coach, what tactical strategies do we need to pay attention to?

E: Based on the characteristics and weaknesses of the opponents, we have to develop corresponding tactics. We need to be flexible and adjust our defensive and offensive strategies accordingly, aiming to control the tempo and initiative of the game. Lastly, regardless of the game's outcome, what matters is that we give our all and perform at our best level.

Remember, team spirit and love for basketball are what drive us to victory.

C: Thank you, Coach! We will train hard and prepare for the game.

E: Excellent! I believe that you will be able to showcase your abilities in the game. Let's give it our all!

E: 大家好！明天我们就要参加重要的篮球比赛了，我想和大家分享一些注意事项和专业要求。

A: 教练，请您告诉我们比赛中需要注意的事项和技巧。

E: 首先，比赛前要进行充分的热身运动，确保身体状态达到最佳状态。这样可以预防运动损伤，并提高身体的灵活性和反应能力。

B: 教练，比赛中有什么技巧需要我们掌握吗?

E: 在比赛中，团队合作是非常重要的。要时刻与队友保持沟通和配合，做好传球和防守的配合。另外，准确的投篮和快速的反应能力也是取胜的关键。

C: 教练，我们有哪些需要注意的战术和策略呢?

E: 针对对手的特点和弱点，我们应制定相应的战术。我们要灵活变化，适时调整防守和进攻的策略，争取掌握比赛的节奏和主动权。最后，不论比赛的结果如何，重要的是我们能够全力以赴，发挥出最好的水平。记住，团队精神和对篮球的热爱是我们胜利的动力。

C: 谢谢教练！我们一定会努力训练，为比赛做好准备。

E: 很好！我相信你们能够在比赛中展现出自己的实力。加油吧！

Unit 4

体育礼仪

Sports Etiquette

在国际体育赛事中，运动员和相关人员需要遵守一定的礼仪规范，包括正式场合下的问候、介绍和礼貌用语等。因此，学习相关的英语表达很有必要。

单词 展示

sportsmanship [ˈspɔːtsmənʃɪp] *n.* 运动员精神，体育道德

respect [rɪˈspekt] *n./v.* 尊重，敬重

fairness [ˈfeənəs] *n.* 公平，公正

etiquette [ˈetɪkət] *n.* 礼仪，规范

integrity [ɪnˈtegrəti] *n.* 正直，诚实

discipline [ˈdɪsəplɪn] *n.* 纪律，自律

teamwork [ˈtiːmwɜːk] *n.* 团队合作，协作

courtesy [ˈkɜːtəsi] *n.* 礼貌，谦恭

grace [greɪs] *n.* 优雅，风度

sportsmanlike [ˈspɔːtsmənlaɪk] *adj.* 有体育精神的，守规矩的

句子示范

During the competition, we should always maintain sportsmanship, respect our opponents, and the referees.

在比赛中，我们应该始终保持体育礼仪，尊重对手和裁判。

Sportsmanship teaches us to approach every game with fairness and refrain from using deceitful tactics to gain an advantage.

体育礼仪教导我们要以公平的态度对待每场比赛，不使用欺骗手段获得优势。

After the game, it is important to show appreciation and congratulate our opponents, regardless of the outcome.

比赛结束后，应该向对手表示赞赏和祝贺，不论胜负。

While watching the game, we should adhere to proper spectator etiquette, avoiding making disruptive noises or interfering with the players.

在观看比赛时，我们要遵守观众的礼仪，不发出嘈杂声音或干扰选手。

在体育课上，老师 Drew 正在教授同学们体育礼仪的重要性和应该注意的事项。

D=Drew　　A=Anna　　C=Cindy　　F=Fergus

D: Students, today we are going to talk about sports etiquette. Sports activities are not just about exercising the body, but also about manners and cooperation. Have you noticed any etiquette issues around you during sports activities?

A: Teacher, what does sports etiquette mean?

D: Sports etiquette refers to the behavior norms of respect, cooperation, and fairness exhibited in sports. It applies not only to competitions but should also be integrated into our daily workouts and sports activities. Now, I will play a video example, and I want you all to watch it and identify any instances that do not comply with sports etiquette.

(*Video plays*)

C: I noticed an issue! One player pushed the opponent, which is not in line with sports etiquette.

D: Very good! Pushing down an opponent is a behavior that violates sports etiquette. In a game, we should respect our opponents, adhere to the rules, and avoid using excessive physical contact.

F: I spotted another issue! After the game, some players did not shake hands with each other but turned away instead.

D: Handshaking is a common etiquette after a sports game. It represents respect for the opponent and signifies a friendly end to the competition. Therefore, regardless of the outcome, we should shake hands with our opponents.

C: Teacher, there's one more issue! In the video, a player mocked the opponent after scoring, which is also against sports etiquette.

D: You're absolutely right! Mocking the opponent is disrespectful and unfriendly behavior. Whether in a game or during regular sports activities, we should adhere to sports ethics, maintaining a friendly and respectful attitude towards others.

D: 同学们，今天我们要谈谈体育礼仪。体育活动不仅仅是锻炼身体，还要注重礼貌和合作。你们在运动中是否注意到身边的礼仪问题呢？

A: 老师，体育礼仪是什么意思呢？

D: 体育礼仪是指在体育运动中表现出来的尊重、合作和公平的行为规范。它不仅仅适用于比赛，也应该贯穿于我们的日常锻炼和体育活动中。现在，我将播放一个视频案例，请同学们观看后找出其中不符合体育礼仪的地方。

（播放视频）

C: 我发现了一个问题！在比赛中，有一个球员推倒了对方，这是不符合体育礼仪的行为。

D: 很好！推倒对手是一种违反体育礼仪的行为。在比赛中，我们应该尊重对手，遵守比赛规则，并避免使用过激的身体接触。

F: 我看到了另一个问题！在比赛结束后，有些球员没有互相握手，而是转身离开。

D: 握手是体育比赛结束后常见的礼仪之一。它代表着对对手的尊重和比赛的友好结束。所以，无论胜负如何，我们都应该与对手握手。

C: 老师，还有一个问题！在视频中，有球员在得分后嘲笑对手，这也是不符合体育礼仪的行为。

D: 你说得对！嘲笑对手是不尊重和不友好的行为。无论是在比赛中还是平时的体育活动中，我们都应该遵守体育道德，对他人保持友善和尊重的态度。

Unit 5

体育赛事

Sports Events

在体育场馆或赛事中，英语常被用作官方语言，用于宣布比赛规则、解释裁判判决以及向观众传达重要信息。对于国际性的体育赛事，英语更是必不可少的工具。下面让我们一起来学习一下吧。

单词 展示

offense [əˈfens] *n.* 进攻，攻势

defensive [dɪˈfensɪv] *adj.* 防守的

training [ˈtreɪnɪŋ] *n.* 训练

outstandingly [aʊtˈstændɪŋli] *adv.* 杰出地

competitiveness [kəmˈpetətɪvnəs] *n.* 竞争力

stadium [ˈsteɪdiəm] *n.* 体育场，运动场

strategy [ˈstrætədʒi] *n.* 战略，策略

intense [ɪnˈtens] *adj.* 强烈的，激烈的

goal [gəʊl] *n.* 目标，得分

score [skɔː(r)] *n.* 比分

句子示范

This swimmer broke the world record.

这个游泳运动员打破了世界纪录。

The athlete got injured during the competition, so he was substituted off the field.

这个运动员在比赛中受伤了，所以被换下场了。

We will participate in an important rugby match tomorrow.

明天我们将参加一场重要的橄榄球比赛。

Their team lost to the opponents in the semi-finals and missed the finals.

他们的球队在半决赛中输给了对手，无缘决赛。

Last night's soccer game was very exciting, and both teams ended up with a draw.

昨晚的足球比赛非常精彩，两支球队打平收场。

Frank 和 George 一起去体育场看了足球赛事，二人针对这场赛事进行了讨论。

F=Frank G=George

G: This match was truly exciting! I think it's one of the most intense games I've ever seen.

F: Absolutely agree! Both teams displayed tremendous competitiveness. Which team do you think performed better?

G: Well, I believe the home team performed outstandingly. Their offense was highly organized, and their passing was precise. The forwards played exceptionally well and played a significant role in scoring goals.

F: You're absolutely right. The home team's offense was indeed impressive. However, I think the away team's defense was also remarkable. They made numerous brilliant saves during the match, especially their goalkeeper. Their defensive line was well-organized, making it difficult to break through.

G: Yes, you're right. I noticed the away team's defensive strategy as well. They worked closely together and didn't give the home team any opportunities. It was truly a game of both strong offense and defense.

F: Were there any particular moments in the match that left a deep impression on you?

G: Definitely! There was one instance when a midfielder from the home team launched an incredible long pass directly to the feet of the forward, who swiftly placed the ball into the opponent's goal. That moment made the entire stadium erupt!

F: I remember that moment! The fans went crazy, including myself. And there was another moment when the away team's forward skillfully dribbled past two defenders and scored a goal. His technique was truly awe-inspiring!

G: Absolutely, they are all true masters of the game. I feel like this match was more than just a game, it was a visual feast. The players' skills, speed, and intelligence were displayed to the fullest on the field.

F: That's absolutely right! This match has indeed left a lasting impression on us.

G: 这场比赛真是精彩！我觉得这是我看过的最激烈的比赛之一。

F: 是的，完全同意！双方队伍都展现出了极强的竞争力。你觉得哪个队踢得更好一些？

G: 嗯，我认为主队表现更出色。他们的进攻非常有组织，传球也相当精准。他们的前锋在比赛中表现得非常出色，进球功不可没。

F: 你说得没错，主队的进攻确实令人印象深刻。但是我觉得客队的防守也非常出色。他们在比赛中做出了许多精彩的扑救，尤其是他们的门将。他们的防线组织得很好，很难攻破。

G: 是的，你说得没错。比赛中，我也注意到了客队的防守策略。他们紧密合作，不给主队任何机会。这真是一场攻守兼备的比赛。

F: 这场比赛中有没有什么特别让你印象深刻的瞬间？

G: 当然有！有一次主队的中场球员发起了一次惊人的长传，直接传到前锋脚下，然后他迅速把球送入了对方球门。那一刻，整个体育场都沸腾了！

F: 我记得那一刻！球迷们都疯狂了，包括我自己。还有一个瞬间是客队的前锋巧妙地过掉了两名防守球员，然后射门得分。他的技术真是令人叹为观止！

G: 是的，他们都是真正的球技高手。我觉得这场比赛不仅仅是一场比赛，更是一场视觉盛宴。球员们的技术、速度和智慧都在场上展现得淋漓尽致。

F: 真的没错！这场比赛确实给我们留下了深刻的印象。

Chapter 7 文化交流

在当今世界，跨国交流与合作日益频繁，各种文化的交汇与碰撞变得常见。而英语口语作为一种全球通用的交流工具，为不同国家和地区的人们架起了友谊的桥梁。学习和使用英语口语，不仅能增加对外国文化的了解，还能向世界展示自己国家的文化和传统。

Unit 1

感受京剧

Listening to the Beijing Opera

京剧是中国传统戏曲艺术的代表，了解和掌握相关的英语表达，可以更好地向他人介绍和传播京剧艺术，让更多的人了解和欣赏到京剧，促进中华文化的传承与交流。

单词展示

stunning [ˈstʌnɪŋ] *adj.* 令人震惊的	spectacular [spekˈtækjələ(r)] *adj.* 引人入胜的
influential [ˌɪnfluˈenʃl] *adj.* 有影响力的	captivating [ˈkæptɪveɪtɪŋ] *adj.* 迷人的
melodious [məˈləʊdiəs] *adj.* 悦耳的	theatrical [θiˈætrɪkl] *adj.* 戏剧的
extensive [ɪkˈstensɪv] *adj.* 广泛的	vividly [ˈvɪvɪdli] *adv.* 生动地，鲜明地
magnificent [mægˈnɪfɪsnt] *adj.* 壮丽的	profound [prəˈfaʊnd] *adj.* 深远的

句子示范

Watching Beijing Opera allows me to immerse myself in a rich atmosphere of traditional culture.

观看京剧表演让我感受到浓厚的传统文化氛围。

Every time I appreciate Beijing Opera, I can feel the unique charm of traditional art.

每一次欣赏京剧，我都能够感受到传统艺术的独特魅力。

Each time I watch Beijing Opera, I am deeply moved by the passionate performances of the actors.

每次看京剧，我都能被演员们高亢激昂的表演所感动。

Li 邀请他的外国朋友 John 去观看京剧演出，并向他介绍了京剧的艺术特点。

L=Li　　J=John

L: Hey, John, what did you think of the Beijing Opera performance?

J: It was truly stunning! I've never seen such a spectacular show before. Beijing Opera is truly a unique art form.

L: I'm glad you liked it! Beijing Opera is one of the most influential forms of traditional Chinese opera. It combines music, dance, vocal performance, and acting, captivating the audience.

J: Yes, I was deeply impressed by the music and vocal performances in Beijing Opera. The actors' voices were melodious, and they were able to convey intense emotions.

L: Absolutely! Beijing Opera has distinctive vocal styles that blend specific tones and unique vocal techniques. Through this approach, the actors can express the emotions and psychological states of their characters.

J: I also noticed their exceptional performance skills. Their body language and facial expressions were incredibly rich, vividly portraying the characters' personalities and emotions.

L: That's one of the performance characteristics of Beijing Opera. The actors undergo extensive training to master the rich techniques of body language and facial expressions, highlighting the characteristics and emotions of their characters.

J: The costumes and makeup in Beijing Opera were also very unique. The actors wore magnificent costumes, appearing as if they had come from ancient times.

L: Absolutely, the costumes and makeup in Beijing Opera are part of its visual allure. They reflect the identities and social status of different characters while enhancing the dramatic and theatrical atmosphere.

J: It was absolutely fantastic! The Beijing Opera performance left a profound impression on me. Thank you for inviting me to watch it and giving me the opportunity to appreciate the cultural treasure of China.

L: I'm delighted that you enjoyed it! Beijing Opera is an integral part of Chinese culture, and I'm honored to share this unique art form with you.

L: 嘿，约翰，你觉得京剧演出怎么样？

J: 真的太震撼了！我从未见过如此精彩的表演。京剧真是一种独特的艺术形式。

L: 我很高兴你喜欢它！京剧是中国传统戏曲艺术中最有影响力的一种。它结合了音乐、舞蹈、唱腔和表演，让人陶醉其中。

J: 是的，我对京剧的音乐和唱腔印象深刻。演员的嗓音非常悦耳，而且他们能够表达出强烈的情感。

L: 没错！京剧有独特的唱腔，它结合了音调和特殊的发声技巧。演员们能够通过这种方式表达角色的情感和心理状态。

J: 我也注意到了他们的精湛表演技巧。他们的身体语言和面部表情非常丰富，能够生动地展现出角色的性格和情感。

L: 这就是京剧的表演特点之一。演员们经过长期的训练，掌握了丰富的身体语言和面部表情的技巧，以突出角色的特点和情感。

J: 京剧的戏服和化妆也非常独特。演员们穿着华丽的服装，看起来像是来自古代。

L: 没错，京剧的戏服和化妆是其视觉魅力的一部分。它们体现了不同角色的身份和社会地位，同时也增添了戏剧性和戏曲的氛围。

J: 真是太棒了！京剧的演出给我留下了深刻的印象。感谢你邀请我观看，让我有机会领略到中国文化的瑰宝。

L: 非常高兴你喜欢！京剧是中国文化的重要组成部分，我很荣幸能与你分享这一独特的艺术形式。

Unit 2

体会书法

Experiencing Calligraphy

书法是中国传统艺术的瑰宝，它以独特的笔法和艺术美感闻名。掌握流利的英语口语将为书法的国际传播提供机会，可以让更多的人了解和欣赏中国书法的魅力。下面让我们一起学习一下吧。

单词展示

inkstone [ˈɪŋkstəʊn] *n.* 砚台，墨砚

inkwell [ˈɪŋkwel] *n.* 墨水瓶，墨汁瓶

scroll [skrəʊl] *n.* 卷轴，纸卷

calligraphy [kəˈlɪgrəfi] *n.* 书法，书法艺术

brushstroke [ˈbrʌʃˌstrəʊk] *n.* 书法笔画

horizontal [ˌhɒrɪˈzɒntl] *adj.* 水平的

vertical [ˈvɜːtɪkl] *adj.* 垂直的

stiff [stɪf] *adj.* 僵硬的

patience [ˈpeɪʃns] *n.* 耐心

intriguing [ɪnˈtriːgɪŋ] *adj.* 有趣的

句子示范

Calligraphy has taught me patience and focus, as each stroke requires careful consideration.

书法教会了我耐心与专注，每一笔都需要仔细斟酌。

The structure and brushstrokes of each character contain profound cultural connotations, deepening my understanding of the aesthetics of Chinese characters.

每个字的结构和笔画都蕴含了深厚的文化内涵，让我对汉字的美学有了更深的理解。

Calligraphy allows me to experience the beauty and power of Chinese characters.

书法让我感受到了汉字的美与力量。

小安带着她的外国朋友 Bob 去体验中国书法，书法王老师教授了他们书法的技巧。

A=An　　B=Bob　　W=Wang

A: Hey, Bob, today I'm taking you to experience Chinese calligraphy. We're going to a calligraphy academy with a renowned calligraphy master. He can teach us the basic techniques of calligraphy.

W: Welcome to learn Chinese calligraphy. Calligraphy is an important part of Chinese traditional culture, emphasizing the strength, speed, and posture of the brushstrokes.

B: I'm curious about the correct way to hold the brush. How should I hold it to create beautiful characters?

W: The correct way to hold the brush is to grip it between the thumb, index finger, and middle finger, maintaining a relaxed and natural hand posture. This ensures stability and fluency in brushstrokes.

B: Wow, the brush looks fascinating! I've never used a brush to write before, so it's a fresh challenge for me.

W: Now, I'll teach you some basic strokes, such as horizontal, vertical, left-falling, and right-falling strokes.

B: Wow, it's much more difficult than I imagined! My characters look a bit stiff.

W: Calligraphy is an art that requires long-term practice and cultivation. It's important to maintain patience and perseverance, and you'll gradually see improvement in your skills.

A: 嘿，鲍勃，今天我带你去体验一下中国书法。我们去的这

家书法学院有一位非常有名的书法老师。他可以教我们书法的基本技巧。

W: 欢迎你们来学习中国书法。书法是中国传统文化的重要组成部分，注重用笔的力度、速度和姿势。

B: 我很想知道如何正确握笔。请问应该怎样握笔才能书写出美丽的字？

W: 正确的握笔方法是将笔夹于拇指、食指和中指之间，保持轻松自然的手部姿势。这样可以保证笔触的稳定性和流畅度。

B: 哇，毛笔看起来很特别！我从未使用过毛笔来写字，这对我来说是一个新鲜的挑战。

W: 现在，我将教你们一些基本的笔画，比如横、竖、撇、捺等。

B: 哇，这比我想象的要难得多！我的字看起来有些生硬。

W: 书法是一门艺术，需要长期的练习和修炼。重要的是保持耐心和恒心，慢慢地你会发现自己的进步。

Unit 3

剪纸活动

Paper-cutting Activity

剪纸是中国民间艺术的重要组成部分，它是以剪刀和纸张为工具创作出精美的艺术作品。与剪纸相关的单词有很多，下面来学习一下吧。

单词展示

scissors [ˈsɪzəz] *n.* 剪刀

template [ˈtempleɪt] *n.* 模板

design [dɪˈzaɪn] *n.* 设计

craft [krɑːft] *n.* 手艺，工艺

cultural [ˈkʌltʃərəl] *adj.* 文化的

exquisite [ɪkˈskwɪzɪt] *adj.* 精致的

artwork [ˈɑːtwɜːk] *n.* 艺术品

originate [əˈrɪdʒɪneɪt] *v.* 起源于

demonstrate [ˈdemənstreɪt] *v.* 演示

fold [fəʊld] *v.* 折叠

句子示范

Participating in paper-cutting activities can cultivate our manual dexterity and creativity while experiencing the joy of art.

参与剪纸活动可以培养我们的动手能力和创造力，体验到艺术的乐趣。

Through paper-cutting, we can appreciate the profound cultural heritage of the Chinese nation.

通过剪纸，我们能够感受到中华民族的深厚文化底蕴。

During paper-cutting activities, we have the freedom to unleash our creativity and design unique paper-cut patterns based on our own ideas.

在剪纸活动中，我们可以自由发挥创意，根据自己的想法设计独特的剪纸图案。

在一座古城，导游 Zhang 带领着一个外国旅行团来到了一个传统手工艺坊，这个手工艺坊专门教授剪纸艺术，导游决定带领他们一起体验剪纸活动。

J=Jimmy　E=Ella　A=Ann　Z=Zhang　P=Peter

Z: Hello, everyone! Welcome to the Chinese paper-cutting workshop. Paper-cutting is one of China's unique traditional crafts, through which we can create various exquisite artworks. Today, I will introduce the history and techniques of paper-cutting and lead you all to experience the joy of this art form.

J: It sounds fascinating! We've never tried paper-cutting before, and we're looking forward to this experience.

Z: Paper-cutting originated in China thousands of years ago. It is a handicraft that uses scissors to cut various patterns on paper. In China, paper-cut artworks often feature auspicious patterns such as flowers, birds, animals, symbolizing happiness and good fortune. Now, please take scissors and paper, and get ready to start your paper-cutting experience.

E: These paper-cut artworks look so exquisite. I'm not sure where to begin.

Z: Don't worry, I'll demonstrate for everyone. First, choose a piece of paper, it can be colored or white, then fold it into half the size of a full sheet. Next, we need to use scissors to cut out the desired patterns on the paper. You can start with simple patterns and gradually increase the difficulty.

A: It seems like this requires a lot of skill and patience. I hope I can create a beautiful piece.

P: This is really fun! I never thought paper-cutting could be so enjoyable. It's a way to interact with traditional culture.

Z: 大家好！欢迎来到中国的剪纸手工艺坊。剪纸是中国独特的传统手工艺之一，通过剪纸，我们可以创作出各种精美的艺术作品。今天我将为大家介绍剪纸的历史和技巧，并带领大家一起体验剪纸的乐趣。

J: 听起来很有趣！我们从未尝试过剪纸活动，期待这个体验。

Z: 剪纸起源于中国，有几千年的历史，它是一种用剪刀将纸张剪出各种图案的手工艺。在中国，剪纸作品常常以吉祥图案为主题，如花鸟、动物等，寓意着幸福和吉祥。现在，请大家拿起剪刀和纸，准备开始剪纸的体验。

E: 这些剪纸作品看起来非常精美。我不知道如何开始。

Z: 不用担心，我将为大家演示一下。首先，选择一张纸，可以是彩色的或白色的，然后将它折叠成半张纸的大小。接下来，我们需要用剪刀将纸张剪出想要的图案。可以先从简单的图案开始，逐渐提高难度。

A: 这听起来好像需要很多技巧和耐心。我希望我能剪出一个漂亮的作品。

P: 这真的很有趣！我以前从未想过剪纸可以如此有意思。这是一种与传统文化互动的方式。

Unit 4

体验刺绣
Experiencing Embroidery

刺绣是中国民间传统手工艺之一，通过针线在织物上刺绣出精美的图案。掌握相关的英语表达，可以让更多的人了解刺绣艺术的独特魅力。下面一起来学习吧。

单词展示

embroidery [ɪmˈbrɔɪdəri] *n.* 刺绣

needle [ˈniːdl] *n.* 针

thread [θred] *n.* 线

fabric [ˈfæbrɪk] *n.* 织物，布料

stitch [stɪtʃ] *n.* 缝合，针脚

vibrant [ˈvaɪbrənt] *adj.* 鲜艳的，充满活力的

texture [ˈtekstʃə(r)] *n.* 质地

essential [ɪˈsenʃl] *adj.* 必要的

intricate [ˈɪntrɪkət] *adj.* 复杂精细的

uniqueness [juːˈniːknəs] *n.* 独特性

句子示范

The embroidery needle in my hand weaves through intricate embroidery patterns, providing me with a unique sense of handmade beauty.

手中的绣针穿梭于细密的绣花图案之间，带给我一种独特的手工艺美感。

In the world of embroidery, I can relax my mind and enjoy the harmonious dance between thread and needle.

在刺绣的世界里，我可以放松心情，享受与线与针的默契舞动。

Through embroidery works, I can sense the inheritance and beauty of ancient culture.

透过刺绣作品，我可以感受到古代文化的传承与美丽。

Every stitch and thread in embroidery embodies the wisdom and patience of artisans, which is truly admirable.

刺绣的每一针每一线都蕴含着工匠的智慧与耐心，让人佩服不已。

小何带着他的外国朋友 Gordon 来到刺绣工坊体验刺绣，刺绣老师马老师为他们讲解了刺绣相关的内容。

H=He　　G=Gordon　　M=Ma

H: Hey, Gordon! Today I'm taking you to experience the beauty of Chinese embroidery. We're going to an embroidery workshop, where we'll meet a highly skilled embroidery teacher. He can teach us some basic embroidery techniques.

G: I'm really excited to get a firsthand experience of embroidery. I've heard that it's a highly intricate craft, and I'm very interested in it.

M: Welcome to the embroidery workshop! I'm delighted to share the wonders of embroidery with you.

G: What materials and tools are needed for embroidery?

M: The main materials for embroidery are silk threads and embroidery fabric. We use high-quality silk threads that are vibrant in color and soft in texture. The embroidery fabric is carefully selected and prepared cotton fabric. Additionally, tools such as embroidery needles and embroidery frames are essential.

G: What is the embroidery master doing?

M: The master is working on an embroidery design. Before starting the embroidery, he transfers the design onto the fabric and uses special embroidery needles to complete the intricate details.

H: Can we try it ourselves?

M: Of course you can.

(*He and Gordon start practicing embroidery under the guidance of the embroidery teacher*.)

M: Very good, you're picking it up quickly! Embroidery requires patience and precise movements. Pay attention to keeping the needle stable and maintaining even stitches.

H: I feel that this kind of handicraft is truly meaningful. Each stitch requires dedication and attention to detail.

G: Absolutely, embroidery is not just a craft, it's a way to express emotions and art.

H: 嘿，戈登！今天我带你来体验一下中国刺绣艺术，我们今天要去刺绣工坊，那里有一位非常有经验的刺绣老师，他可以教我们一些刺绣的技巧。

G: 真是期待能够亲眼看到刺绣的制作过程！听说刺绣是一门非常精细的手工艺，我很感兴趣。

M: 欢迎你们来到刺绣工坊！我很高兴能与你们分享刺绣的

美妙。

G: 刺绣需要什么样的材料和工具呢？

M: 刺绣的主要材料是丝线和绣布。我们使用优质的丝线，颜色鲜艳，质地柔软。而绣布则是经过精心挑选和处理的高质量棉布。此外，绣针、绣架等工具也是必不可少的。

G: 这位刺绣师傅在做什么呢？

M: 这位师傅正在进行刺绣的设计。在开始刺绣之前，他会根据设计稿将图案转移到绣布上，并使用特殊的刺绣针来完成细节部分。

H: 我们可以体验一下吗？

M: 当然可以。

（小何和戈登开始跟着马老师的示范，慢慢地练习刺绣。）

M: 很好，你们掌握得很快！刺绣需要耐心和细致的动作。注意保持绣针的稳定和线迹的均匀。

H: 我觉得这样的手工艺真的很有意义。每一针每一线都需要用心去完成。

G: 是的，刺绣不仅仅是一种手工艺，更是一种表达情感和艺术的方式。

Unit 5

领略希腊神话

Appreciating of Greek Mythology

希腊神话是世界文化遗产之一，而提升英语口语表达能力可以更深入地了解和欣赏这些古老的神话故事，全面地了解西方文化。下面让我们一起学习与希腊神话相关的表达吧。

单词展示

Zeus [zjuːs] *n.* 宙斯

Poseidon [pəˈsaɪd(ə)n] *n.* 波塞冬

Aphrodite [ˌæfrəˈdaɪti] *n.* 阿佛洛狄忒

Apollo [əˈpɒləʊ] *n.* 阿波罗

Athena [əˈθiːnə] *n.* 雅典娜

preside [prɪˈzaɪd] *v.* 统治，主持

abode [əˈbəʊd] *n.* 住所

Greek [griːk] *adj.* 希腊的

mythology [mɪˈθɒlədʒi] *n.* 神话学

mural [ˈmjʊərəl] *n.* 壁画

句子示范

Aphrodite, the goddess of beauty and love in Greek mythology, is captivating with her beauty and allure.

希腊神话中的阿佛洛狄忒是美与爱的女神，她的美貌和魅力令人倾倒。

Exploring the Olympus Mountain, you will discover the abode of numerous gods and goddesses in Greek mythology.

探索奥林匹斯山脉，你会发现希腊神话中众多神祇的居所。

Poseidon, the god of the sea, reigns over the power of the oceans and earthquakes in Greek mythology.

海洋之神波塞冬在希腊神话中掌管着海洋和地震的力量。

Hera, in Greek mythology, is not only the wife of Zeus but also the goddess of marriage and family.

希腊神话中的赫拉不仅是宙斯的妻子，也是婚姻和家庭的女神。

博物馆进行希腊神话的展览，讲解员 Miranda 给同学们

讲解希腊神话相关内容，让同学们领略了神话的魅力。

M=Miranda N=Nana S=Selena

M: Welcome to the Greek Mythology Exhibition Area! Here, we will explore the magnificent world of ancient Greek mythology. First, let's take a look at this mural depicting Zeus ruling Mount Olympus.

N: Wow! This scene is truly breathtaking! Is Zeus really the king of the gods?

M: Yes, Zeus is the king of the gods in Greek mythology. He presides over the power of the sky and thunder. Mount Olympus is the abode of the gods, and Zeus reigns over them there.

S: Who are these other gods? What magical powers do they possess?

M: In addition to Zeus, there are gods like Poseidon, the god of the sea, Athena, the goddess of wisdom and warfare, Aphrodite, the goddess of love and beauty, and many more. Each god has their unique divine powers and attributes, governing their respective domains.

N: I've heard of Pandora, who is she? Is there a story about her here?

M: Of course! Pandora is a female figure in Greek mythology. She opened Pandora's box, releasing various calamities and misfortunes, but in the end, only hope remained in the box.

N: These mythological stories are truly fascinating! I find the characters and stories in Greek mythology very interesting, and they sometimes provide us with insights.

S: Absolutely!

M: 欢迎来到希腊神话展览区！在这里，我们将领略古希腊神话的壮丽世界。首先，我们看到的这幅壁画，它描述的是宙斯统治奥林匹斯山的场景。

N: 哇！这画面真是太震撼了！宙斯真的是众神之王吗？

M: 是的，宙斯是希腊神话中的众神之王，他掌管着天空和雷电的力量。奥林匹斯山是众神的居所，宙斯就在这里统治着众神。

S: 那这些其他的神是谁？他们都有什么神奇的能力？

M: 除了宙斯，还有海神波塞冬、智慧战争女神雅典娜、爱与美的女神阿佛洛狄忒等。每个神都有自己独特的神力和属性，用来统领各自的领域。

N: 我听说过潘多拉，她是谁？这里有关于她的故事吗？

M: 当然有！潘多拉是希腊神话中的一个女性形象。她开启了潘多拉魔盒，释放了各种灾难和不幸，但最后只剩下希望在盒子里。

N: 这些神话故事真是精彩纷呈！我觉得希腊神话中的人物和故事都很有意思，它们有时候可以给我们一些启示。

S: 确实如此！

Unit 6

体味西餐

Tasting Western Food

西餐在世界各地广受欢迎，通过学习英语，我们可以更好地理解和体验西餐的烹饪技巧、餐桌礼仪以及背后的文化与历史。下面让我们一起学习一下关于西餐的英语表达吧。

单词展示

steak [steɪk] *n.* 牛排

pasta [ˈpæstə] *n.* 意大利面食

pizza [ˈpiːtsə] *n.* 比萨饼

burger [ˈbɜːɡə(r)] *n.* 汉堡包

salad [ˈsæləd] *n.* 色拉

cuisine [kwɪˈziːn] *n.* 烹饪，菜肴

menu [ˈmenjuː] *n.* 菜单

choices [ˈtʃɔɪsɪz] *n.* 选择

appetizer [ˈæpɪtaɪzə(r)] *n.* 开胃菜

grilled [ɡrɪld] *adj.* 烤的

句子示范

Through savoring Western cuisine's seasonings, I have discovered the diverse layers that different ingredients and spices can create.

通过细细品味西餐的调味，我发现不同的配料和香料可以产生出丰富的层次感。

While enjoying Western dishes, I not only taste the delicacies but also feel the cultural and social ambiance at the dining table.

享用西餐的过程中，我不仅品尝到美食，还能感受到餐桌上的文化与社交氛围。

In the process of savoring Western cuisine, I gradually explore the uniqueness of food cultures in various countries and regions.

在品味西餐的过程中，我逐渐发现了不同国家和地区饮食文化的独特之处。

Western cuisine emphasizes delicate cooking techniques and artistic plating, making each dish a gustatory and visual delight.

西餐注重细腻的烹饪技巧和摆盘艺术，每一道菜都是一种味觉和视觉的享受。

Millie 带中国朋友 Lucy 来到西餐厅，品尝西餐的味道，并讲述了一些关于西餐的知识。

M=Millie　　L=Lucy

M: Lucy, welcome to this Western restaurant! Today, I'm going to treat you to an authentic Western meal and let you experience it firsthand.

L: Thank you, Millie! I'm looking forward to trying the taste of Western cuisine. The menu here seems to have a lot of choices. Could you give me an introduction?

M: Of course! The menu for Western cuisine is typically divided into several sections, such as appetizers, main courses, and desserts. Appetizers are usually small-sized starters, such as salads, soups, or seafood. Main courses typically include options like meat, fish, pasta, and fried rice. Desserts are the final course of the meal and can be cakes, ice cream, or fruits, among others.

L: Wow, it sounds so lavish! I'd like to try an appetizer and a main course. Do you have any recommendations?

M: The Caesar salad is a classic choice for an appetizer in Western cuisine. It consists of fresh vegetables and a flavorful Caesar dressing. As for the main course, steak is a popular choice for many people. You can choose between a grilled or slightly rare steak, depending on your preferred texture.

L: Alright, let's order a Caesar salad and a grilled steak then! What about drinks?

M: Right, the restaurant offers a variety of drink options, including soft drinks, juices, coffee, and red wine.

(*After the dishes are served*)

M: Hmm, it looks delicious! Let's start savoring the Western cuisine.

L: This Caesar salad is indeed special, with fresh vegetables and a tasty dressing. And it's my first time trying a grilled steak, it's tender and flavorful!

M: I'm glad you enjoyed it! Western cuisine is a unique culinary culture, and I hope through this experience, you'll gain a better understanding and appreciation for it.

M: 露西，欢迎来到这家西餐厅！今天我要带你尝尝正宗的西餐，一起体验一下吧！

L: 谢谢你，米莉！我很期待尝试西餐的味道。这里的菜单好像有很多选择，你能给我介绍一下吗？

M: 当然！西餐的菜单通常分为几个部分，比如开胃菜、主菜和甜点。开胃菜一般是一些小份的前菜，比如沙拉、汤或者海鲜。主菜通常包括肉类、鱼类、面食和炒饭等选择。甜点就是一餐的最后一道菜，可以是蛋糕、冰淇淋或者水果等。

L: 哇，听起来很丰盛！我想试一下开胃菜和主菜。你有什么推荐吗？

M: 开胃菜中的恺撒沙拉是西餐中非常经典的选择，它有新鲜的蔬菜和香味浓郁的沙拉酱。而主菜中的牛排是很多人喜欢的选择，可以选择煎烤或者烤得稍微生一点的口感。

L: 好的，那我们就点一个恺撒沙拉和一份煎牛排吧！还有饮料呢？

M: 对，西餐厅的饮料有很多选择，包括软饮料、果汁、咖啡和红酒等。

（上菜后）

M: 嗯，看起来很美味！让我们开始品味西餐吧。

L: 这个恺撒沙拉确实很特别，蔬菜新鲜，搭配的酱汁很好吃。而且我第一次尝试煎牛排，它的口感很嫩，味道很香！

M: 很高兴你喜欢！西餐是一种独特的美食文化，希望你能通过这次体验更加了解和喜欢它。

Chapter 8 前沿科技

随着社会的不断发展，科技也在迅速发展，很多前沿科技开始出现，有的已经在生活中被广泛使用。科技的发展必然会催生新的科技概念和词语，掌握与之相关的英语表达，可以更好地了解和从事前沿科技，所以学习前沿科技方面的英语表达很有必要。

Unit 1

人工智能

Artificial Intelligence

人工智能是一门涉及算法、机器学习和数据分析的前沿学科。与之相关的英语表达有很多，下面就一起来学习一下吧。

单词 展示

artificial [ˌɑːtɪˈfɪʃl] *adj.* 人工的

intelligence [ɪnˈtelɪdʒəns] *n.* 智能

algorithm [ˈælgərɪðəm] *n.* 算法

neural [ˈnjʊərəl] *adj.* 神经的

network [ˈnetwɜːk] *n.* 网络

deep [diːp] *adj.* 深度的

reinforcement [ˌriːɪnˈfɔːsmənt] *n.* 强化

language [ˈlæŋgwɪdʒ] *n.* 语言

processing [ˈprəʊsesɪŋ] *n.* 处理

recognition [ˌrekəgˈnɪʃn] *n.* 识别

句子示范

Do you know how artificial intelligence mimics human thinking?

你知道人工智能是如何模仿人类思维的吗？

Artificial intelligence can help us process large amounts of data more quickly.

人工智能可以帮助我们更快地处理大量的数据。

Artificial intelligence has great potential in the field of healthcare, assisting doctors in making more accurate diagnoses.

人工智能在医疗领域有很大的潜力，可以辅助医生进行更准确的诊断。

While artificial intelligence has many advantages, we also need to use it with caution to avoid unforeseen issues.

虽然人工智能有很多优势，但我们也需要谨慎使用，避免出现不可预测的问题。

A公司举办了人工智能产品展览，主持人 Henry 回答了

参观者的相关问题。

C=Cora D=Donald E=Edwin H=Henry

H: Hello everyone! Welcome to this exhibition on artificial intelligence! Our company is dedicated to developing various AI products, and today we will showcase a few of them. First, let me introduce our voice assistant, AI Voice.

C: Hello, may I ask how AI Voice is different from other voice assistants?

H: AI Voice utilizes advanced natural language processing technology and deep learning algorithms, which give it higher accuracy and intelligence in speech recognition and semantic understanding. It can comprehend complex instructions, perform tasks, and adapt to the user's needs.

D: That sounds impressive! Does AI Voice support multiple languages?

H: Yes, AI Voice supports multiple languages, including English, Chinese, French, and Spanish, among others. We continuously optimize and expand its speech recognition and translation capabilities to provide a better user experience.

E: Besides the voice assistant, do you have any other products?

H: Absolutely! We have also developed an intelligent home control system called AI Home. It seamlessly integrates with various smart devices and home systems, allowing you to control lighting, temperature, security, etc. by using voice commands or a mobile application.

C: That sounds very exciting!

H: 大家好！欢迎来到这次人工智能展览！我们的公司致力于开发各种人工智能产品，今天我们将为您展示其中的几款产品。首先，让我向大家介绍我们的语音助手 AI Voice。

C: 您好，请问 AI Voice 与其他语音助手有何不同之处？

H: AI Voice 采用了先进的自然语言处理技术和深度学习算法，使其在语音识别和语义理解方面具有更高的准确性和智能化。它能够理解复杂的指令，执行任务，并且能够个性化适应用户的需求。

D: 听起来很厉害！那么，AI Voice 能够支持多种语言吗？

H: 是的，AI Voice 支持多种语言，包括英语、中文、法语和西班牙语等。我们不断优化和扩展语音识别和翻译功能，以提供更好的用户体验。

E: 除了语音助手，您还有其他产品吗？

H: 当然！我们还开发了一款智能家居控制系统，名为 AI Home。它能够与各种智能设备和家居系统进行无缝连接，通过语音或手机应用控制家中的照明、温度、安全等方面。

C: 听起来非常令人期待！

Unit 2

新能源

New Energy

在新能源领域，掌握更多与之相关的英语表达十分有必要，因为这样可以帮助我们加深对新能源的了解，促进在这一领域的合作与交流。下面就一起来学习与新能源相关的表达吧。

单词展示

renewable [rɪˈnjuːəbl] *adj.* 可再生的

energy [ˈenədʒi] *n.* 能源

solar [ˈsəʊlə(r)] *adj.* 太阳能的

wind [wɪnd] *n.* 风能

hydroelectric [ˌhaɪdrəʊɪˈlektrɪk] *adj.* 水力发电的

biomass [ˈbaɪəʊmæs] *n.* 生物质能源

sustainable [səˈsteɪnəbl] *adj.* 可持续的

emission [ɪˈmɪʃn] *n.* 排放

geothermal [ˌdʒiːəʊˈθɜːml] *adj.* 地热的

energy-efficient [ˈenədʒi ɪˈfɪʃnt] *adj.* 能源高效的

句子示范

We should actively promote the use of renewable energy to reduce reliance on fossil fuels.

我们应该积极推广新能源的利用，以减少对化石燃料的依赖。

Solar energy is a common form of renewable energy that can be converted into electricity to power our homes and industries.

太阳能是一种常见的新能源，它可以转化为电力供应我们的家庭和工业用电。

The importance of new energy lies in its ability to reduce dependence on traditional fossil fuels while reducing environmental pollution.

新能源的重要性在于它可以减少对传统化石能源的依赖，同时减少环境污染。

B 公司为了寻求发展，准备开拓新能源领域，项目负责人 Amy 向经理 Donald 做了相关的报告。

A=Amy　　D=Donald

A: Manager, I have completed the report on our exploration of the new energy sector, and I would like to share it with you.

D: Which types of new energy did you mention in the report?

A: We have researched solar energy, wind energy, and geothermal energy among other types of new energy. Solar energy is an infinite renewable resource that converts sunlight into electricity through photovoltaic effects. Wind energy utilizes wind power to rotate wind turbines and generate electricity. Geothermal energy, on the other hand, utilizes the heat energy deep within the Earth's crust for power generation and heating purposes.

D: How are the prospects for these new energy sources?

A: The development of new energy sources holds immense market potential. The global demand for renewable energy is continually increasing, and governments around the world are encouraging the use of renewable energy to combat climate change. Additionally, the ongoing technological advancements and cost reductions in new energy technologies present us with excellent business opportunities.

D: Very well. I believe you can organize a team and initiate this project.

A: 经理，我完成了关于我们开拓新能源领域的报告，我想与您分享一下。

D: 你在报告中提到了哪些新能源类型？

A: 我们研究了太阳能、风能和地热能等新能源类型。太阳能是一种无限可再生的能源，通过光电效应将太阳能转化为电能。风能利用风力转动风力发电机产生电能。而地热能则利用地壳深处的热能来发电和供暖。

D: 这些新能源的发展前景如何？

A: 发展新能源具有巨大的市场潜力。全球对可再生能源的需求不断增加，各国政府也在鼓励使用可再生能源以应对气候变化。此外，新能源技术的不断进步和成本的降低也为我们提供了良好的商机。

D: 好的。我认为你可以组织团队，启动这个项目了。

Unit 3

AR 技术

AR Technology

AR 技术是一种融合虚拟信息和现实世界的技术。与这项技术有关的英语表达你知道多少呢？下面就来学习一下与 AR 技术相关的英语表达吧。

单词展示

augmented [ɔːgˈmentɪd] *adj.* 增强的

reality [riˈæləti] *n.* 现实

virtual [ˈvɜːtʃuəl] *adj.* 虚拟的

environment [ɪnˈvaɪrənmənt] *n.* 环境

interactive [ˌɪntərˈæktɪv] *adj.* 互动的

hologram [ˈhɒləgræm] *n.* 全息图

projection [prəˈdʒekʃn] *n.* 投影

gesture [ˈdʒestʃə(r)] *n.* 手势

overlay [ˈəʊvəˈleɪ] *n.* 叠加

simulation [ˌsɪmjuˈleɪʃn] *n.* 模拟，仿真

句子示范

Recently, our company has introduced AR technology to provide users with a more immersive experience.

最近我们公司引入了 AR 技术，为用户提供更加沉浸式的体验。

With AR technology, we can overlay virtual information onto the real world.

通过 AR 技术，我们可以将虚拟信息叠加在现实世界中。

We plan to incorporate AR features into our new product to enhance user experience.

我们计划在新产品中加入 AR 功能，以提升用户体验。

C 公司欲与 B 公司合作研发 AR 技术应用，C 公司派来项目经理 Vincent 与 B 公司技术顾问 Maria 探讨有关 AR 技术方面的问题。

V=Vincent　　M=Maria

V: Hello, I'm the project manager from Company C. We highly appreciate your company's expertise in AR technology, and we would like to collaborate with you in developing an AR application.

M: Thank you very much for your recognition of our company. AR technology has a wide range of applications, and I believe our collaboration will yield excellent results. Do you have specific project requirements?

V: We are planning to develop an AR application for the education sector, aiming to help students learn and understand scientific knowledge better. We would like to leverage B Company's technical strengths to create an innovative and engaging product.

M: This is a promising project. Applying AR technology in the education sector can provide interactive learning experiences and assist students in mastering knowledge. I'd like to know more about your specific requirements for product features and user experience.

V: We hope this AR application can provide diverse science simulations and virtual demonstrations, allowing students to participate and experience them firsthand through AR technology. Additionally, we also want to offer personalized learning paths and feedback mechanisms to cater to different students' needs.

M: Okay.

V: Thank you very much for your suggestions and answers! Next, we can further discuss specific cooperation details and establish a timeline.

V: 你好，我是 C 公司的项目经理。我们对贵公司在 AR 技术方面的实力非常赞赏，我们希望能与你们合作开发一款 AR 应用。

M: 非常感谢您对我们公司的认可。AR 技术的应用领域非常广泛，我相信我们的合作会取得很好的成果。您有具体的项目需求吗？

V: 我们计划开发一款针对教育领域的 AR 应用，用于帮助学生更好地学习和理解科学知识。我们希望能够结合 B 公司的技术优势，打造一个创新且有趣的产品。

M: 这是一个很有前景的项目。在教育领域应用 AR 技术，可以提供互动式的学习体验，帮助学生更好地掌握知识。我想了解一下您对产品功能和用户体验有哪些具体的要求？

V: 我们希望这个 AR 应用能够提供多样化的科学模拟实验和虚拟演示，让学生可以通过 AR 技术参与其中，亲身体验。同时，我们也希望能够提供个性化的学习路径和反馈机制，以满足不同学生的需求。

M: 好的。

V: 非常感谢您的建议和解答！接下来，我们可以进一步商讨具体的合作细节和时间计划。

Unit 4

元宇宙

Metaverse

元宇宙是虚拟现实技术的进一步发展，创建了一个全球虚拟的互联网络空间。与元宇宙相关的英语表达十分丰富，下面就一起来学习一下吧。

单词展示

metaverse [ˈmetəvɜːs] *n.* 元宇宙

avatar [ˈævətɑː(r)] *n.* 头像

digital [ˈdɪdʒɪtl] *adj.* 数字的

blockchain [blɒktˈʃeɪn] *n.* 区块链

decentralized [ˌdiːˈsentrəlaɪzd] *adj.* 分散的

expansion [ɪkˈspænʃn] *n.* 扩展

virtualization [ˈvɜːtʃʊəˌlaɪzeiʃən] *n.* 虚拟化

experience [ɪkˈspɪriəns] *n.* 经验

comprehensive [ˌkɒmprɪˈhensɪv] *adj.* 全面的

句子示范

I look forward to the metaverse bringing more immersive virtual experiences to people.

我期待着元宇宙能够为人们带来更多沉浸式的虚拟体验。

In the metaverse, people can interact with others through digital avatars representing themselves.

在元宇宙中，人们可以通过数字化的头像代表自己与他人交互。

Blockchain technology plays a crucial role in the metaverse, ensuring data security and traceability.

区块链技术在元宇宙中起着重要的作用，确保数据的安全和可追溯性。

Through the metaverse, people can achieve cross-temporal socialization and collaboration.

通过元宇宙，人们可以实现跨时空的社交和协作。

A 公司准备做元宇宙相关的项目，便请来 Amy 老师为

员工进行培训。

A=Amy　C=Cindy　B=Bob

A: Hello everyone! Welcome to the metaverse training course. I am your instructor. Today, we will explore the concept and applications of the metaverse. First, let's understand what the metaverse is.

C: Teacher, what exactly is the metaverse? I'm not very familiar with this concept.

A: The metaverse is a virtual digital world that consists of digital content, virtual reality technology, and interactive experiences. In the metaverse, people can create, interact, and experience various content and activities in a digitized form.

B: What are the application scenarios of the metaverse? What does it mean for our company?

A: The metaverse has a wide range of application scenarios. It can be applied in fields such as education, entertainment, business, and social interactions. For our company, the metaverse can provide additional interactive ways for our products, create more immersive experiences for customers, and also open up new business opportunities.

C: I heard that the metaverse is related to virtual reality. What is the difference between them?

A: That's correct. The metaverse is related to virtual reality but is not exactly the same concept. Virtual reality refers to a completely virtual environment created through technology, where users can be fully immersed. The metaverse, on the other hand, is a more comprehensive and open concept. It includes virtual reality but also encompasses other digital content and user interactions.

A: 大家好！欢迎来到元宇宙培训课程。我是你们的培训老师。今天，我们将探索元宇宙的概念和应用。首先，让我们来了解一下什么是元宇宙。

C: 老师，元宇宙到底是什么？我对这个概念还不太了解。

A: 元宇宙是一个虚拟的数字世界，它由数字内容、虚拟现实技术和人们的交互共同构成。在元宇宙中，人们可以以数字化的形式创造、交互和体验各种内容和活动。

B: 元宇宙有什么应用场景呢？它对我们的公司有什么意义？

A: 元宇宙的应用场景非常广泛。它可以应用于教育、娱乐、商业、社交等领域。对于我们公司来说，元宇宙可以为我们的产品提供更多的交互方式，为客户创造更加沉浸式的体验，同时也为我们拓展新的商业机会。

C: 我听说元宇宙和虚拟现实有关系，它们有什么区别？

A: 没错，元宇宙和虚拟现实是相关但不完全相同的概念。虚拟现实是指通过技术创造出的一种完全虚拟的环境，用户可以完全沉浸其中。而元宇宙是一个更加综合和开放的概念，它包含了虚拟现实，但也包括了其他的数字内容和用户交互。

Unit 5

6G 技术

6G Technology

6G 技术是下一代移动通信技术，涉及尖端的无线通信和网络科技。掌握与 6G 技术相关的英语表达十分重要，下面就来学习一下相关的英语表达吧。

单词展示

wireless [ˈwaɪələs] *adj.* 无线的

network [ˈnetwɜːk] *n.* 网络

connectivity [ˌkɒnekˈtɪvəti] *n.* 连接性

speed [spiːd] *n.* 速度

latency [ˈleɪtənsi] *n.* 延迟

bandwidth [ˈbændwɪdθ] *n.* 带宽

holography [hɒˈlɒgrəfi] *n.* 全息照相术

beamforming [ˈbiːmfɔːmɪŋ] *n.* 波束成形

cybersecurity [ˌsaɪbəˌsɪˈkjʊərəti] *n.* 网络安全

privacy [ˈprɪvəsi] *n.* 隐私

句子示范

6G technology will bring faster network speeds and lower latency.

6G 技术将带来更快的网络速度和更低的延迟。

6G will accelerate the popularization and application of edge computing.

6G 将加速边缘计算的普及和应用。

The advent of 6G will drive the development of the Internet of Things and Artificial Intelligence.

6G 的到来将推动物联网和人工智能的发展。

C 公司正在开发 6G 技术相关的项目，但项目进展一直不顺利，于是项目负责人 Bonny 便召集大家一起开会。

B=Bonny　　L=Linda　　J=Jack

B: Hello everyone, thank you for attending this meeting. As we all know, the 6G technology project we have developed has been facing challenges and making slow progress. I hope to hear your thoughts and suggestions today to find solutions to the problems.

L: Yes, the project has encountered many challenges. I believe we need a deeper understanding of the core elements of 6G technology, in order to better address the issues.

J: I agree, we need to enhance the team's technical capabilities. We can consider adopting more advanced antenna technologies and signal processing algorithms to improve data transmission speed and latency. At the same time, we can optimize network architecture and transmission protocols to enhance overall performance.

B: What are others' views on the challenges of 6G technology?

L: The advent of 6G technology will provide us with higher transmission speeds and lower latency, which will be a breakthrough for our communication products. We can connect smart devices to the 6G network to achieve more intelligent and interconnected smart home solutions.

B: Absolutely!

B: 大家好，谢谢你们参加这次会议。我们都知道，我们开发的 6G 技术项目一直进展不顺利。我希望今天能够听到你们的想法和建议，找到解决问题的办法。

L: 是的，项目目前遇到了很多挑战。我觉得我们需要更深入地了解 6G 技术的核心要素，以便更好地应对问题。

J: 我同意，我们需要加强团队的技术能力。我们可以考虑采用更先进的天线技术和信号处理算法来改善数据传输速度和延迟。同时，我们也可以优化网络架构和传输协议，以提高整体性能。

B: 其他人对 6G 技术的挑战有何看法?

L: 6G 技术的到来将为我们提供更高的传输速度和更低的延迟，这对于我们的通信产品来说将是一大突破。我们可以将智能设备与 6G 网络连接，实现更智能化和互联互通的智能家居解决方案。

B: 没错!

Unit 6

数字化办公

Digital Office

数字化办公是现代企业普遍采用的管理模式，掌握与之相关的英语表达，可以使工作开展得更顺利。下面就来学习一些有关数字化办公的英语表达吧。

单词展示

digitalization [ˌdɪdʒɪtəlaɪˈzeɪʃn] *n.* 数字化

productivity [ˌprɒdʌkˈtɪvəti] *n.* 生产力

automation [ˌɔːtəˈmeɪʃn] *n.* 自动化

collaboration [kəˌlæbəˈreɪʃn] *n.* 协作

workflow [ˈwɜːkfləʊ] *n.* 工作流程

efficiency [ɪˈfɪʃnsi] *n.* 效率

integration [ˌɪntɪˈɡreɪʃn] *n.* 集成

communication [kəˌmjuːnɪˈkeɪʃn] *n.* 通信

e-signature [ˈiː sɪɡnətʃə(r)] *n.* 电子签名

database [ˈdeɪtəbeɪs] *n.* 数据库

句子示范

Digitalization of office work improves work efficiency and team collaboration.

数字化办公提高了工作效率和团队协作能力。

Digitalization of office work solves the problem of traditional paper document management.

数字化办公解决了传统纸质文件管理的问题。

Cloud computing technology provides strong support for digitalization of office work.

云计算技术为数字化办公提供了强大的支持。

Mobile apps enable employees to work anytime and anywhere.

移动应用程序使员工能够随时随地进行办公工作。

A 公司最近正在推进数字化办公，总监 Dan 召集人力资源经理 Cindy、市场经理 Benny、财务经理 Emily 一起召开会议商讨策略。

D=Dan　　C=Cindy　　B=Benny　　E=Emily

D: Hello everyone! Thank you very much for attending today's meeting. We need to discuss our digital office strategy.

B: We can use digital channels and tools to more accurately target customers and effectively promote our products.

C: We can implement an electronic recruitment system and online training platforms to enhance recruitment efficiency and employee development.

E: We can adopt digital accounting software and online reimbursement systems to enhance the accuracy and efficiency of financial data processing.

D: So let's create an implementation plan for digitalization, clearly defining specific tasks and timelines for each department. We need to maintain communication and collaboration throughout the implementation process.

B: We should ensure that we train our employees to adapt to the digital work environment. Training and skills development are key to the success of digital transformation.

C: I agree. We should also pay attention to employee feedback and engagement to ensure the smooth progress of digitalization.

E: Lastly, we need to consider the costs and budget of digitalization. We should establish a clear understanding of the relationship between investment and returns, as well as the costs associated with long-term maintenance and updates.

D: 大家好！非常感谢你们来参加今天的会议。我们需要商讨一下我们的数字化办公策略。

B: 我们可以通过数字化渠道和工具，更精确地定位目标客户，并有效地推广我们的产品。

C: 我们可以实施电子招聘系统和在线培训平台，提高招聘效率和员工发展。

E: 我们可以采用数字化会计软件和在线报销系统，提高财务数据的准确性和处理效率。

D: 那么让我们制订一个数字化办公的实施计划，明确每个部门的具体任务和时间表。我们需要在实施过程中保持沟通和协作。

B: 我们应该对员工进行培训，使他们适应数字化办公环境。培训和技能提升是数字化转型成功的关键。

C: 我同意。我们还应该关注员工的反馈和参与度，确保数字化办公的顺利推进。

E: 最后，我们需要考虑数字化办公的成本和预算。我们应该明确投入和回报的关系，以及长期维护和更新的费用。

Unit 7

3D 打印

3D Printing

3D 打印技术（three-dimensional Printing）是一种快速制造技术，与此相关的英语表达非常多，下面就来一起学习吧。

单词 展示

layer [ˈleɪə(r)] *n.* 层

prototype [ˈprəʊtətaɪp] *n.* 原型

slicing [ˈslaɪsɪŋ] *n.* 切片

nozzle [ˈnɒzl] *n.* 喷嘴

resin [ˈrezɪn] *n.* 树脂

raft [rɑːft] *n.* 基座

support [səˈpɔːt] *n.* 支撑物

thickness [ˈθɪknəs] *n.* 厚度

printer [ˈprɪntə(r)] *n.* 打印机

parameter [pəˈræmɪtə(r)] *n.* 参数

句子示范

I am learning 3D printing technology, which can create complex three-dimensional objects.

我正在学习 3D 打印技术，它可以制造出复杂的立体物体。

We can use 3D modeling software to design our products.

我们可以使用 3D 建模软件来设计我们的产品。

3D printing technology can reduce material waste and is environmentally friendly.

3D 打印技术可以减少材料浪费，对环境友好。

This model needs to be printed with a 3D printer.

这个模型需要使用 3D 打印机打印出来。

Gordon 刚刚入职公司，对于 3D 打印技术还不熟悉，Judy 作为老员工正在为他提供帮助。

G=Gordon　　J=Judy

J: Hello, Gordon! I heard that you're not very familiar with 3D printing technology. Do you need any help?

G: Yes, I'm not quite familiar with how it works and its applications.

J: 3D printing is a technology that creates three-dimensional objects by layering materials one layer at a time. First, we use computer-aided design (CAD) software to create a 3D model.

G: Oh, I know CAD software. It's used to design various objects.

J: That's right. Once the model is designed, we need to convert it into the STL file format, which is a standard format for 3D printing.

G: Got it.

J: Next, we load the STL file into the 3D printer and select the appropriate printing parameters, such as the printing material, layer thickness, and printing speed, etc. Then, the printer will layer the materials one by one to print the 3D model into a physical object.

G: That sounds great! I'm looking forward to learning and understanding more about 3D printing technology now.

J: 你好，戈登！我听说你对 3D 打印技术还不太了解，需要帮助吗？

G: 是的，我对它的工作原理和应用领域不太清楚。

J: 3D 打印技术是一种通过逐层堆叠材料来制造三维物体的技术。首先，我们需要使用计算机辅助设计软件创建一个 3D 模型。

G: 噢，我知道 CAD 软件，它可以用来设计各种物体。

J: 对的。在设计好模型后，我们需要将它转换为 STL 文件格式，这是一种用于 3D 打印的标准格式。

G: 明白了。

J: 接下来，我们将 STL 文件加载到 3D 打印机中，并选择合适的打印参数，例如打印材料、层厚度和打印速度等。然后，打印机会逐层堆叠材料，将 3D 模型打印成实体物体。

G: 这听起来很棒！我现在更加期待学习和了解更多关于 3D 打印技术的知识了。

参考文献

[1] 陈的非，刘朝晖 . 饭店实用英语 [M]. 北京：机械工业出版社，2008.

[2] 陈国亭，仲艳琴，魏绪 . 精编交流英语 [M]. 哈尔滨：哈尔滨工业大学出版社，2007.

[3] 郝绍伦 . 金融英语（第 2 版）[M]. 合肥：中国科学技术大学出版社，2009.

[4] 金敬红 . 研究生英语口语教程（上）[M]. 沈阳：辽宁教育出版社，2003.

[5] 金利 . 每天 10 分钟日常英语口语 [M]. 北京：化学工业出版社，2016.

[6] 李龙，何忠家 . 职业英语口语 [M]. 北京：中国铁道出版社，2014.

[7] 李文昊，杨琪主编，易人外语教研组编著 . 英语口语 900 句：速记活用全新版 [M]. 南京：江苏凤凰科学技术出版社，2016.

[8] 李玉萍，李文 . 实用商务英语综合教程：中级 [M]. 北京：人民邮电出版社，2012.

[9] 刘荷清 .365 天英语会话“袋”着走 . 旅游英语 [M]. 北京：中

国纺织出版社，2019.

[10] 马永红 . 留学英语 [M]. 北京：中国科技大学出版社，2009.

[11][英] 尼克 · 斯特克（Nick Stirk）著，王青译 . 商务英语写作王 [M]. 长沙：湖南文艺出版社，2017.

[12][英] 萨默斯著 , 管燕红等编译 . 朗文英语写作活用词典：英汉双解 [M]. 北京：商务印书馆，2012.

[13] 盛丹丹 . 商务英语步步赢 [M]. 北京：国防工业出版社，2010.

[14] 唐智霞，李慧娟 . 新编商务英语口语教程 [M]. 郑州：大象出版社，2009.

[15] 王继辉 . 奥运会英语口语读本：高级本 [M]. 北京：北京师范大学出版社，2007.

[16] 张艳秋，浩瀚 . 职场英语口语倒背如流 [M]. 北京：机械工业出版社，2009.

[17] 中国国际贸易学会商务专业培训考试办公室 . 跨境电商英语教程 [M]. 北京：中国商务出版社，2016.

[18] 钟亚捷 . 超实用商务英语大全集 [M]. 南京：江苏凤凰科学技术出版社，2020.